D0891414

LUKE-ACTS
AND THE
JEWISH PEOPLE

*Eight
Critical Perspectives*

——————*Edited by*——————

JOSEPH B. TYSON

AUGSBURG Publishing House • Minneapolis

LUKE-ACTS AND THE JEWISH PEOPLE
Eight Critical Perspectives

Copyright © 1988 Augsburg Publishing House

Scripture quotations, unless translated by the author directly from the Greek or Hebrew, are from the Revised Standard Version of the Bible, copyright 1946, 1952, and 1971 by the Division of Christian Education of the National Council of Churches.

Library of Congress Cataloging-in-Publication Data

Luke-Acts and the Jewish people: eight critical perspectives / edited by
  Joseph B. Tyson.
      p. cm.
    "Several of the papers were originally delivered in Atlanta in
  1986 at the annual meeting of the Society of Biblical Literature's
  Group on Acts"—Pref.
    Bibliography: p.
    Contents: The Church of God and Godfearers / Jacob Jervell—
  "Glory to thy people Israel": Luke-Acts and the Jews / David L.
  Tiede—The ironic fulfillment of Israel's glory / David P.
  Moessner—The Jewish people in Luke-Acts / Jack T. Sanders—
  Insider or outsider?: Luke's relationship with Judaism / Marilyn
  Salmon—Rejection by Jews and turning to Gentiles: the pattern of
  Paul's mission in Acts / Robert C. Tannehill—The mission to the
  Jews in Acts: unraveling Luke's "Myth of the 'myriads' " / Michael
  J. Cook—The problem of Jewish rejection in Acts / Joseph B.
  Tyson.
    ISBN 0-8066-2390-X
    1. Bible. N.T. Luke—Criticism, interpretation, etc. 2. Bible.
  N.T. Acts—Criticism, interpretation, etc. 3. Jews in the New
  Testament. 4. Judaism (Christian theology)—Biblical teaching.
  I. Tyson, Joseph B. II. Society of Biblical Literature. Group on
  Acts. Meeting (1986 : Atlanta, Ga.)
  BS2589.L83 1988
  226'.4—dc19   88-13765
                                                             CIP

Manufactured in the U.S.A.   APH 10-4132

1   2   3   4   5   6   7   8   9   0   1   2   3   4   5   6   7   8   9

CONTENTS

CONTRIBUTORS

Michael J. Cook is Professor of Intertestamental and Early Christian Literatures at Hebrew Union College—Jewish Institute of Religion, Cincinnati, Ohio. Among his recent articles are "The Ties that Blind: II Corinthians 3:12ff.," in *When Jews and Christians Meet*, ed. John J. Petuchowski (Albany: State University of New York Press, 1988), and "Confronting New Testament Attitudes on Jews and Judaism: Testing Four Jewish Perspectives," *Chicago Theological Seminary Register* 78 (1988).

Jacob Jervell has been Professor of New Testament Exegesis and Theology at the University of Oslo since 1960. He has been visiting professor at Yale, Aarhus, and Lund Universities. He is the author of twelve books on Luke-Acts, including *Luke and the People of God* (Augsburg, 1972) and *The Unknown Paul* (Augsburg, 1984).

David P. Moessner is Associate Professor of New Testament Language, Literature, and Exegesis at Columbia Theological Seminary, Decatur, Georgia. His book, *Lord of the Banquet: The Literary and Theological Significance of the Lukan Travel Narrative,* will soon appear.

Marilyn Salmon is Assistant Professor of Scripture at the College of St. Catherine, St. Paul, Minnesota. She holds the Ph.D. degree from Hebrew Union College—Jewish Institute of Religion; her dissertation was titled, "Hypotheses about First-Century Judaism and the Study of Luke-Acts."

Jack T. Sanders is Professor of Religious Studies at the University of Oregon in Eugene. One of his most recent publications is *The Jews in Luke-Acts* (SCM; Fortress, 1987).

Robert C. Tannehill is the Fred D. Gealy Professor of New Testament at the Methodist Theological School in Ohio, Delaware, Ohio. His most recent book is *The Narrative Unity of Luke-Acts: A Literary Interpretation,* volume 1: *The Gospel according to Luke* (Fortress, 1986).

David L. Tiede is President and Professor of New Testament at Luther Northwestern Theological Seminary in St. Paul, Minnesota. He is the author of *Prophecy and History in Luke-Acts* (Philadelphia: Fortress, 1980) and of *Augsburg Commentary on the New Testament: Luke* (Augsburg, 1988).

Joseph B. Tyson is Professor of Religious Studies at Southern Methodist University in Dallas, Texas. His most recent book is *The Death of Jesus in Luke-Acts* (University of South Carolina Press, 1986).

ABBREVIATIONS

Commonly used periodicals, reference works, and serials

AB	Anchor Bible
AnBib	Analecta biblica
BARev	*Biblical Archaeology Review*
BETL	Bibliotheca ephemeridum theologicarum lovaniensium
Bib	*Biblica*
BZ	*Biblische Zeitschrift*
BZNW	Beihefte zur Zeitschrift für die neutestamentliche Wissenschaft
CBQ	*Catholic Biblical Quarterly*
CII	*Corpus inscriptionum iudicarium*
FRLANT	Forschungen zur Religion und Literatur des Alten und Neuen Testaments
HNT	Handbuch zum Neuen Testament
HTR	*Harvard Theological Review*
HTS	Harvard Theological Studies
HUCA	*Hebrew Union College Annual*
IDB	G. A. Buttrick, ed., *Interpreter's Dictionary of the Bible*
Int	*Interpretation*
JAC	Jahrbuch für Antike und Christentum
JAOS	*Journal of the American Oriental Society*
JBL	*Journal of Biblical Literature*
JR	*Journal of Religion*
JSJ	Journal for the Study of Judaism in the Persian, Hellenistic and Roman Period
NovT	*Novum Testamentum*
NovTSup	Novum Testamentum, Supplements
NTD	Das Neue Testament Deutsch
NTS	*New Testament Studies*
PWSup	Supplement to Pauly-Wissowa, *Real-Encyclopädie der classischen Alterumswissenschaft*
RB	*Revue Biblique*
RevExp	*Review and Expositor*
RNT	Regensburger Neues Testament
SANT	Studien zum Alten und Neuen Testament
SBLDS	Society of Biblical Literature Dissertation Series
SBLMS	Society of Biblical Literature Monograph Series
SNTSMS	Society for New Testament Studies Monograph Series

Str-B	H. Strack and P. Billerbeck, *Kommentar zum Neuen Testament*
TDNT	*Theological Dictionary of the New Testament* (trans. of *TWNT*)
THKNT	Theologischer Handkommetar zum Neuen Testament
TQ	*Theologische Quartalschrift*
TS	*Theological Studies*
TWNT	G. Kittel and G. Friedrich, eds. *Theologisches Wörterbuch zum Neuen Testament*
WMANT	Wissenschaftliche Monographien zum Alten und Neuen Testament
ZNW	*Zeitschrift für neutestamentliche Wissenschaft*

Ancient literature

Ant.	Josephus, *Antiquities of the Jews*
b.Ned.	Babylonian Talmud, tractate *Nedarim*
b.Yebam.	Babylonian Talmud, tractate *Yebamot*
Jub.	The Book of Jubilees
2 Bar.	2 Baruch
Sib. Or.	Sibylline Oracles
T. Levi	Testament of Levi, Testaments of the Twelve Patriarchs
T. Simeon	Testament of Simeon
y.Bik.	Jerusalem Talmud, tractate *Bikkurim*

PREFACE

In recent decades issues relating to the treatment of Jews in early Christian literature have been vigorously discussed among New Testament scholars, church historians, Christian theologians, and Judaic scholars. Indeed, these issues have been debated with a passion that is not usually associated with these scholarly disciplines. Implicit in the discussion is a recognition that a great deal is at stake for contemporary relationships between Christians and Jews, for the documents in question are not only widely influential in modern society, but for many they carry the highest weight of authority. If it is true that, as Rosemary Ruether (*Faith and Fratricide: The Theological Roots of Anti-Semitism* [New York: Crossroad, 1974]) and others have claimed, anti-Judaism is deeply rooted in the New Testament, Christians and Jews both must find some ways of dealing with this phenomenon and its implications.

The present volume constitutes an attempt to trace the treatment of Jewish people and institutions in one set of New Testament texts, the Gospel of Luke and the book of Acts. Several of the papers were originally delivered in Atlanta in 1986 at the annual meeting of the Society of Biblical Literature's Group on Acts. At this session an attempt was made to afford scholars opportunities to present quite varied views on the subject at hand. Three major presentations, each paired with a response, were given, all of which are included here. The paper by David L. Tiede was paired with the response by David P. Moessner; that of Jack T. Sanders with the response by Marilyn Salmon; and the essay by Robert C. Tannehill received a response from Michael J. Cook. Two additional chapters have been included in this volume, namely, those of Jacob Jervell and Joseph B. Tyson.

The reader should not expect to find here a single thesis, such as might be found in a monograph. Rather, this volume attempts to explore the manifold issues and perspectives, some of which are unabashedly contradictory, held by scholars who may be considered experts in Luke-Acts. The volume, then, should be seen as a contribution to the ongoing discussion of the treatment of Jews in Luke-Acts, not as an attempt to bring the discussion to a halt.

In agreement with the vast majority of New Testament critics, the scholars represented in this volume agree that Luke and Acts came from the hand of the same author. Thus the essays will generally draw on both documents. Nevertheless, most of the attention will be directed toward the book of Acts, since most of the material that bears on the problems addressed here comes from this book. It must be kept in mind, however, that the authors represented here are sensitive to certain themes that may be traced in both books; thus frequent reference to the Gospel of Luke may be expected.

Although there is no single thesis to be found in the various readings, it may be good for the reader to be alert to some of the major issues in the discussion. One issue that is addressed in a variety of ways is that of the nature of the Christian mission to Jews as pictured in Acts. The book begins with some portraits of the Christian community in Jerusalem. In these portraits it is clear that the community is a Jewish-Christian one that is experiencing marked growth. But later in the book there are many signs of Jewish rejection of the Christian message and of an increasing leaning of the Christian movement toward Gentiles. The reader may thus ask what Luke intends to be understood by this kind of presentation. Does he suggest that Jewish rejection of the gospel is final? Does he mean that, after Paul's last speech to the Jews at the end of Acts, there is to be no more Christian mission to the Jews? Does he think of this Jewish rejection as tragic? Is it in some way a fulfillment of Old Testament promises regarding Israel? Or does Luke promote a fundamentally negative attitude toward the Jews, one that would regard them as rejected by God because of their rejection of the Christian message? These problems are addressed, in a variety of ways, by Cook, Moessner, Sanders, Tannehill, Tiede, and Tyson.

A related issue is that of Luke's intended audience. If Luke is himself a Gentile, writing for a predominantly Gentile audience, his treatment of the Jews is likely to be understood in a negative way. If, however, he and his audience share a Jewish heritage, his books should be read in a way similar to the way Paul's letters are read.

In this context, even Luke's seemingly negative statements take on a different color. Salmon deals directly with this issue, but it appears also in some of the other chapters.

A third issue that has a major bearing on the entire complex of problems is that of the so-called Godfearers. Luke mentions this group of people a number of times in Acts, and he understands them as Gentiles who have made a limited commitment to Judaism. Jacob Jervell maintains here that the Christian mission in Acts is directed *only* to Godfearing Gentiles and to Jews. There is no question of a mission to pagans. If Jervell is right, the whole question of Luke's treatment of the Jewish people vis-à-vis the Gentiles takes on a different character.

The chapter by Jack T. Sanders, "The Jewish People in Luke-Acts," previously appeared in a slightly revised version in his book, *The Jews in Luke-Acts* (London: SCM; Philadelphia: Fortress, 1987), and is used here by permission of the publishers.

The chapter by David L. Tiede, "'Glory to Thy People Israel': Luke-Acts and the Jews," is published also in *The Social World of Formative Christianity and Judaism: Essays in Tribute to Howard Clark Kee*, ed. Jacob Neusner et al. (Philadelphia: Fortress, 1988), and is used by permission of the publisher.

The editor would like to express his gratitude not only to the contributing authors but also to James S. Bury and Ann S. Wilson, whose professional and technical assistance has been invaluable.

Joseph B. Tyson

1

THE CHURCH OF JEWS AND GODFEARERS

Jacob Jervell

A cts has often been seen as the most important document for the Gentile mission within early Christianity. It shows the movement of the church away from Israel and to the Gentiles. Very seldom, however, do we find studies about what kinds of Gentiles Luke is talking about, and thus on the question whether there actually is a movement from Israel to the Gentiles. To Jews in antiquity Gentiles are far more than one, unspecified group. There are proselytes, that is, former Gentiles, and there are Godfearers,[1] and separated from both are the "pure" Gentiles, the *goyim*.

It is far from the truth to talk about Luke favoring Gentiles as the members of the church. Luke's church consists primarily of Christian Jews, the heirs of Israel.[2] And the Gentiles of Acts are a very special group of Gentiles, more semi-Jews than Gentiles,[3] if there is something like a semi-Jew[4] (surely there is, in actuality if not in theory). Luke has no mission to pagans, only to Gentiles. He does not welcome to the church Gentiles of the kind regularly to be found in Jewish Scriptures: the idolaters and people without knowledge of the Torah and its precepts, the enemies of God and Israel. Such Gentiles, "pure" Gentiles, we do not find in the church of Luke. At most they are very rare exceptions. When Paul deals with such Gentiles—and they are the core of his church—he warns them against becoming more like Jews or semi-Jews; cf. 1 Cor. 7:17ff., "Every one should remain in the state in which he was called." Luke has a different policy. The "pure" Gentiles, the pagans, are

11

in his eyes not fit for the kingdom of heaven—as if he himself was a Jew.

The types of Gentiles who, according to Luke, belong to the church are exclusively those who may be called Jewish Gentiles.[5] That means proselytes, whom Luke does not often mention and, above all, the so-called Godfearers or worshipers of God, that is, people with strong ties to Israel and the Law, who are members of the synagogue but are not circumcised.[6]

It has often been noticed that the Godfearers play a significant role in Acts. The mission among them is seen as a step toward the "full" Gentiles. But Luke does not take that step in Acts. If the Godfearers are Luke's own invention, this is not our problem.[7] Luke's idea about them is clear anyway. I find it hard to believe that the Godfearers did not play an important role in Judaism in Luke's time. Be that as it may, to Luke the Godfearers are a significant part of the synagogues.[8] And precisely these so-called Godfearing Gentiles are the only Gentiles he finds and wants to find in the church. For only so can the church hold up its claim to be the true and only Israel of God. The Godfearers don't make the Jews of the church unclean as other Gentiles do. Luke sees a great and decisive difference between them and the other Gentiles, because they are allowed to participate in the worship of the synagogue.[9] And if there are Gentiles who want to become members of the church without being Godfearers, they have to become *phoboumenoi* in order to become Christians. For "pure" Gentiles—pagans—the church is not open. And when such people hear the gospel, they reject it. So the Jews cannot object to the church being the true Israel by referring to the Gentiles. Then the church deals with the Gentiles the same way the Jews themselves do, or at least should have done according to the Scriptures.

The church's Gentile is Cornelius, Acts 10–11. He has all the characteristics of the Godfearers, namely, *eusebēs, phoboumenos ton theon,* praying to God always and giving much alms to the people, that is, Israel (Acts 10:2,22). The almsgiving particularly shows him as devoted to Israel and wanting to have a part in the people of God (10:2,4,31).[10] Almsgiving means to turn to the people and confess one's fellowship with them. So if he is not religious, in the more general meaning of the word, then his behavior toward Israel is the core of his piety. This can be seen from the fact that

Cornelius is "acknowledged by the whole Jewish nation" (Acts 10:22; cf. Luke 7:10ff.). The first Gentile in the church is recommended by the Jews.[11] To Luke, Cornelius is far more than the first Gentile to become Christian. He is the model, the prototype for every non-Jew who wants to be a member of the church. This is seen first from Acts 11:18—the conversion of Cornelius means that God has granted repentance to the Gentiles. Moreover, we have Acts 15:7. At the apostolic council Peter tells how God made the choice that the Gentiles by his mouth should hear the gospel and believe. This refers to the Cornelius episode. He is more than an individual, because he represents *ta ethnē*. When James at the same meeting mentions "a people from the Gentiles for his name" (15:14, my translation), he refers to the words of Peter (15:7) and so to Cornelius. This people of God consists of Godfearers. Further, this is demonstrated from Acts 10:35.[12] Peter draws the conclusion from the Cornelius story: acceptable to God in every nation, *en panti ethnei,* is the man who is Godfearing, *phoboumenos,* and does righteousness, *dikaiosynē. Dikaiosynē* and almsgiving to Israel are one and the same thing.[13] Acts 10:35 does not signal some sort of universalism in our meaning of the word, but points to a very specific group of people. First, Luke uses the technical word for "Godfearers," *ho phoboumenos theon.* Second, he talks about a specific Jewish piety when mentioning "righteousness," as *dikaiosynē* in this part of Acts above all means almsgiving (see Acts 10:2; cf. 10:35). Third, the word *dektos,* "accepted," is a word from the cultic sphere. And fourth, the expression "in every nation" does not mean "every nation," since Israel is exempted, and this meaning may be clearly seen from Acts 10:36-37, 41–42. Luke uses in Acts *pan ethnos* or *panta ta ethnē* for Gentiles. That "God is no respecter of persons" (10:34) is true only in respect to the relation between Israel and the nations, the Gentiles. But it does not put all the Gentiles on the same footing. Only the Godfearers within the nations are acceptable to him, that is, besides Israel.

And so the old problem of the connection of Acts 10:34f., being seen as a universalistic statement, and 10:35ff., with its "nationalistic" tone, is no problem whatsoever. The same goes for the apparent lack of connection between the situation and the sermon. But this is no more strange than the situation in the synagogue with its mixed audience of Jews and Godfearers. The same idea lies behind the Cornelius story. The Godfearers are incorporated in the true Israel. So when Luke here talks about the Godfearers in 10:35, the statement is made with the presupposition of the exclusion of other Gentiles.

So far the picture of the church is given. It consists of Jews, the most pious Jews, as can be seen from the notices of mass conversions.[14] In addition there are, not Gentiles, but Godfearers. In that sense the church is very much like the synagogue, where you find the same two groups.[15] The difference, however, is clear. Then the Godfearers become full partners when it comes to salvation. They are saved in the same way as the Jews are (Acts 15:7ff.). But the Gentiles of the church are throughout of a kind the synagogues could accept, or, according to Luke, ought to accept.

We can follow the prototype of Cornelius throughout Acts, and we will have confirmed the idea of the Gentiles of the church being the Godfearers.

Acts 11:20 mentions the first step toward a Gentile mission undertaken in Antioch. Some of the men who were scattered after the persecution in Jerusalem began to speak even to the Gentiles, the *Hellēnas*.[16] That this means Godfearers[17] is clear not only from 10:2, 35; Luke uses the word *Hellēn* in Acts to signify Godfearers (Acts 14:1; 17:4; 18:4; 19:19,17; 21:21).

The same idea goes through the mission undertaken by Paul. Paul is sent to Jews and Gentiles (Acts 26:18), the last ones being throughout Acts again the Godfearers. In his first missionary speech, in Pisidian Antioch, Paul meets two groups, and he meets them in the worship of the synagogue: the Israelites and the Godfearers, the *phoboumenoi ton theon* (13:16,26). He addresses the two groups as one audience. Both groups belong to the synagogue. And the words of Paul are words to the people Israel (13:15). This does not mean that the Godfearers are Israelites, but they belong in some way to the people. That Paul's sermon is successful is demonstrated in 13:43: many of the Jews and of the *sebomenōn prosēlytōn* followed him and became believers. The strange expression *sebomenōn prosēlytōn* can only mean Godfearers, which is clear from 13:48. The only mission undertaken in Antioch is this one among Jews and Godfearers. The connection between the two groups is testified to in Acts 13:50. The Jews undertake actions against Paul together with the Godfearers, in this case the outstanding women. The same thing happens in Iconium (14:1). A large body of Jews and Greeks, again Godfearers as this happens in the synagogue,[18] became believers. Other Gentiles start a persecution against the missionaries (14:2,5). So far in the account of Acts Luke can conclude, in the form of a report from Paul, that God had opened the door of faith unto the Gentiles, *panta ta ethnē*, which signifies nothing but Godfearers (Acts 14:27). This must be true even of the governor Sergius Paulus (13:7ff.). Then Paul's missionary preaching in Cyprus takes place only in the synagogues (13:5). That Sergius Paulus is a worshiper of God is clear not only from what is said about the church's Gentiles in the prototype Cornelius (10:2,4,22,35). But Sergius Paulus has with him a Jewish prophet, Bar Jesus, who is, however, a sorcerer (13:6). And Sergius Paulus is characterized as an *anēr synetos*, which does not mean that he is intelligent, but—from the Septuagint—a man "showing insight," that is, pious, Godfearing. Luke would not call any pagan *synetos*. And when Sergius Paulus wants to hear the "word of God," *logos tou theou*, this means to Luke always the Scriptures that are attached to the synagogue (13:5; cf. 13:15, 44, 46-48; 17:13; cf. 13:10).[19]

The demands to the Gentiles at the apostolic council are of a kind which could be directed to Godfearers: they must be circumcised (Acts 15:1). That is the one thing Cornelius is not (10:28; 11:3). When to this Acts 15:5 adds the requirement to keep the Law of Moses, the meaning is that they must keep the whole Law and not only parts of it. Thus, the people in question, namely, the Godfearers, already keep parts of the Law. What Peter refers to in Acts 15:7 is meant the same way; the *panta ta ethnē* are people worshiping God. The apostolic decree (15:19,21) is in the right place in this context. The decree has been seen as a contradiction to what is said in Acts 10–11, where no demand whatsoever is given to the Gentiles. There is unconditional, free allowance. The situation in Acts 15 is different,[20] as the Gentiles here will have to keep parts of the Law. But there is no problem here. It is not necessary to demand that Cornelius keep the regulations of the decree, since he already lives by such rules (10:2,4,22,36). But in Acts 15 Luke will show what kinds of Gentiles there are in the church. What is said in the decree is to Luke exactly the same as what is said by Moses in the synagogue (15:21).[21] The saying in 15:21 is unproblematic when the Gentiles are seen as Godfearers. And the church is like a synagogue, giving the right message to the Gentiles.

After the apostolic council, the mission undertaken is seen as in the first part of Acts. The Lydia of Philippi is *sebomenē ton theon* (Acts 16:14), and this is the only missionary effort in this city. The pagan citizens of Philippi bring the missionaries before the magistrates in order to have them punished. In Thessalonica some Jews from the synagogue were converted (17:2-4a), as were a great number of Godfearers (17:4b). The influential women mentioned in this connection are obviously Godfearers too (17:4b). This is clear from the report from Beroea (17:10-12). In addition to the Jews from the synagogue receiving the gospel, there is a great number of Greeks, Godfearers, "women of standing as well as men." The same goes for Athens as well (17:17).

A new situation is in view in Corinth (Acts 18:5-11). When Paul has to leave the synagogue because of the disbelief of the Jews, he continues his work among the Godfearers. He proclaims that he is going to the Gentiles (18:6) and does so by preaching in a house next door to the synagogue, the house belonging to Titius Justus, a worshiper of God, *sebomenou ton theon* (18:7).[22] The two sayings in 13:46 and 18:6 mean exactly the same thing: Paul turns from the Jews to the Godfearers. As we shall see, this goes even for 28:28. So the picture is consistently the same: the church consists of Jews and Godfearers. And the many who are God's people in Corinth, *laos polys* (18:10) have the same composition as we have seen so far in Acts.

The last missionary report comes from Ephesus. Paul preaches here for two years, and it is repeated: to Jews and *Hellēnas,* which can only mean Godfearers (Acts 19:10).[23] In his farewell speech in Miletus, Paul is summing up his work among Jews and Godfearers, *Hellēsin* (20:21). And this is concluded in his report to James and the elders in Jerusalem. He talks about what God has done through him among the Gentiles, *en tois ethnesin* (21:18-26). First, it has to do with Gentiles living among Jews, because Paul's work among Gentiles at the same time means preaching to the Jews (21:21), which is meaningful in a synagogal setting. Second, these Gentiles are seen from the view that they keep parts of the Torah. For this is the meaning of mentioning the apostolic decree in this context.

The church is a church of Jews and semi-Jews. But what about the pagans, the Gentiles who are not Godfearers? There is, of course, at least one report of a conversion where it is not clear whether we have to do with a worshiper of God. That is the jailer in Philippi (Acts 16:27ff.). Nothing is said about his status at all, so he could be a "pure" Gentile. After the presentation of Cornelius as prototype, we would expect that even the jailer belonged to that group, but we cannot be sure.

All the reports of mass conversions have to do only with Godfearers, apart from the Jews:

- Acts 11:21: a great number, *polys te arithmos;*
- Acts 13:43: many, *polloi;*
- Acts 14:1: a great crowd, *poly plēthos:*
- Acts 17:4: a great crowd, *plēthos poly;*
- Acts 18:6: many, *polloi;*
- Acts 18:10: many people, *laos polys.*

But there is not a single word about the same missionary results among Gentiles other than Godfearers. So what then about the pagans in Acts?

First, something should be said about Luke's notions of paganism.[24] These notions are truly Jewish. First and foremost, all paganism is idolatry (Acts 14:11, 15; 17:16, 22ff.). The Gentiles worship idols. These idols are partly shaped by human craftmanship and design (7:44; 17:24, 29; 19:24ff.). The worship of idols can be in the form of worshiping man, as when Herod lets himself be greeted as a god, usurping the honor due to God (12:22ff.). In Beroea Paul and Barnabas are called Mercury and Jupiter, and the people want to offer sacrifice to them (14:13). There is idolatry even in the figure of Simon Magus (8:10). Idolatry is the most shameful thing also in the history of Israel (7:39ff.). Even eating meat offered to idols is branded as idolatry (15:20, 29; 21:25). Idols are nothing but follies (14:15), worthless and powerless things compared to God the creator. Idolatry comes from ignorance (17:30). The church confronts this paganism too. The difference from the attitude towards the church's Gentiles, the worshipers of God, is clear. There are no missionary efforts taken when it comes to these Gentiles, e.g., those people who hail Herod as god (12:22). In meeting with and preaching to such pagans, the preaching is without any effect, if they preach to them at all. We will have to reconsider our ideas of Acts. Generally the mission among the Jews is seen by modern critics as a failure, whereas the church has great success among Gentiles, often with reference to Acts 13:46; 18:6; 28:28. However, against the idea of the fruitless work among Jews we have the notices of mass conversions (2:41; 4:4; 5:14; 6:1,7; 9:42; 12:24; 13:43; 14:1; 17:10ff.; 21:20). As for the great success among Gentiles, this is true only insofar as it applies to Godfearers. But the pagans are not being converted. Paul and Barnabas are horrified when the people of Lystra try to offer sacrifices to them as if they were gods (14:7ff.). To Luke the missionary preaching is always very powerful, but not among pagans. There is in the Lystra episode an exhortation to conversion from pagan follies (14:15), but not a single conversion takes place.[25] Throughout the story we can feel Luke's abhorrence. He ends the story with the laconic words that the missionaries barely managed to prevent the crowd from offering sacrifice (14:18), an account that takes the place of the usual report on great results. Such idolaters do not belong to the church. We notice also that the usual reference to Israel and the people of God is missing (see 10:34ff.). And the speech here given by Peter is the prototype of a missionary sermon to Gentiles, that is, Godfearers. It is not found in Acts 14. This is the reason why the people in Lystra are not worshipers of God and have nothing at all to do with Israel. The short sermon in 14:14-17 is not a missionary proclamation to Gentiles. It is more an apologetic dissociation from paganism. The typical missionary sermon is found in 10:34ff. and 13:16ff. There is but one type, because the content of the sermon applies both to Jews and Gentiles, i.e., Godfearers.

Neither is the Areopagus speech (Acts 17:16-31) a sermon,[26] but more like a discourse or a lecture on true and false religion. The readers of Acts would have no edification from it. We notice even here Luke's abhorrence. Acts 17:16 tells us about the Jewish wrath against idolatry.[27] The tension between 17:16 and 17:22 clearly is there,[28] but if anything is to be labeled Lukan it is obviously 17:16. Nothing from 17:16 is withdrawn in 17:22,[29] and even within the speech there are sharp criticism and complaints against paganism (17:29-30). Paganism is nothing but sinful, false religiosity only to be condemned. The only possibility—and it is remote—of something else lies in the "unknown God" (17:23).

As in Lystra, the efforts in Athens are in vain. As in Lystra, Paul is forced into a situation where he speaks to pagans. In Athens some scoffed, others wanted another discourse at another time (Acts 17:32). Luke gives the opinion of the whole audience in 17:32— *hoi men . . . hoi de.* And he closes the scene in 17:33—Paul left the assembly.

There is, however, in Acts 17:34, a short addition about some people, *tines,* becoming believers. The sentence in 17:34 is obviously the conclusion of Paul's whole stay in Athens (Acts 17:16ff.). We are told that he as usual preached in the synagogues to Jews and Godfearers (17:17), but there is no mention here of any results; Luke postpones mentioning the results until Acts 17:34. The few persons mentioned in 17:34 are obviously not from the Areopagites or philosophers assembled to hear Paul. For among them there is a woman, Damaris, and Luke knows that Paul spoke only to men at the Areopagus (17:22). And among the believers there is only one from the assembly at the Areopagus, Dionysius. In any case the results are very meager. These kinds of people, of Gentiles, at the Areopagus, are not the Gentiles of the church. If we would talk about a few rare exceptions, even of enlightened Gentiles, to the rule that the church consists of Godfearers, it does not alter the picture of the church of Jews and Gentile worshipers of God.

Luke concludes his report by talking about the Gentiles: to them salvation has been sent; they will listen (Acts 28:28). The situation here is different from the former parts of Acts. For now the last and conclusive word about Israel has been said (28:25-27). Acts 13:46 and 18:6 should not be understood as the end of Paul's mission to the Jews. After 13:46 Paul goes to other synagogues (Acts 14–18), and after 18:6 he leaves the synagogue in Corinth but continues his work among Godfearers and Jews (18:7-8). By Acts 28 he has come to the end with the Jews. This is said clearly through the quotation of Isa. 6:9f. in Acts 28:26-27. The true Israel is gathered, as far as the Jews go (cf. 15:15-18). Now the mission will go further, but solely to the Gentiles (28:28). What kinds of Gentiles? Exactly the same as Luke has dealt with throughout his work: the Godfearers. There is no sign whatsoever in Acts that Luke now talks of another audience. The confident words of 28:28, "They will listen. . . ," are substantiated by all the synagogue scenes from Acts 13 forward. The words refer to the Godfearers. Only they have shown a willingness to listen to the gospel. The confidence, if directed to pagans, is baseless when we consider the clash with paganism in Acts 14:8ff.

and 17:22ff. Those people did not listen. The Godfearers are no step on the route to the "pure" Gentiles. And the notion that the mission could reach the Godfearers even outside the synagogue is clear from 18:6ff.

It is not difficult to see why the idea about exactly this composition of the Christian church is so important to Luke. It has to do with his idea of the church as the only and true Israel of God, the legitimate heir of the promises and salvation. Therefore Luke is eager to show that the church consists of "real" Law-pious Jews.[30] To their piety no objection is possible (Acts 21:20).[31] Further, the Gentiles in the church are precisely the kinds of Gentiles who already are present and accepted in the synagogues. Luke saw no objections to their taking part in the life of the synagogue. They did not threaten or diminish the holiness of Israel. Why then the holiness of the church? These worshiping Gentiles are even mentioned in the Scriptures (Acts 15:15ff.). The difference from the synagogue is this: they are given the full unrestricted and unlimited part in that which belongs to Israel: salvation.

I do not think that Luke had any idea that he could convince synagogal Jews about the legitimacy of the church as the true Israel. But he surely could address himself to those important people in the church who came from the synagogue. At this time they still played an important role in the church.[32] And the Gentiles should know about the legitimacy of their inheritance.

2

"GLORY TO THY PEOPLE ISRAEL": LUKE-ACTS AND THE JEWS

David L. Tiede

I. CHRISTIAN HISTORY AND JUDAISM

Luke-Acts is a Jewish-Christian story that fell into Gentile hands. From at least as early as the second century, Luke's history of the beginnings of the Christian movement has been read as an account of the triumph of Gentile Christianity at the expense of Judaism. In developing its myth of Christian beginnings,[1] normative Christianity has regularly interpreted this narrative as foundational to its claim of having displaced Israel as heir to God's promises. The apostolic speeches in Acts calling for repentance have become standing Christian indictments of Jewish complicity in Jesus' death and of the refusal of the Jews to be converted by Christian proclamation of the gospel.[2]

The stakes are high in the current discussion of Luke's view of the Jewish people and their leaders, and it would be foolish to attempt even a historical study of the text without recognizing the pervasive influence which anti-Judaism has so long had in Christian theology and New Testament interpretation.[3] It would also be absurd to seek to disguise the uncompromising declarations Luke-Acts makes concerning Jesus, as if divisions in Israel which the followers of this

Messiah further provoked were inconsequential. The stakes were high in the last third of the first century too.

Nevertheless, the sociology and identity of the first-century author and readers were significantly different from the communities of subsequent interpreters. Because recent critical scholarship has been able to challenge long-established traditions of reading Luke-Acts,[4] the questions at stake in Luke's context may again be pursued carefully and distinguished from the issues of the use which has been made of the text. Even the identification of the author simultaneously with Israel and with this messianist movement has become credible. Critical history and literary studies have shed new light on the context and content of Luke's story as a tale told within the history of Israel rather than at the expense of "the Jews."

Recent historical research into first-century Jewish history has certainly raised more questions than it has answered, but it has successfully challenged the monolithic structures of "normative Judaism" and "apostolic Christianity" which had been erected by interpreters of the first century and have so long served the dogmatic interests of both subsequent traditions. In place of idealized images of the origins of each heritage, which could always be used as foils for the denigration of the other tradition, both the Pharisaic and messianist movements are now depicted as taking shape within a much more complex and diverse religious, cultural, political, and social context. The reconstructed past within which the Luke-Acts narrative may be read has changed.

In the decades surrounding the destruction of the second temple, several alternative traditions, subcultures, and methods of being "true Israel" were still actively competing.[5] In Luke-Acts, the Pharisees are regarded as the major contenders with the messianist movement for the claim to be true Israel, and the charges of apostasy have become mutually acrimonious between these Jewish groups (see Acts 3:23; 21:21). Nevertheless, even these charges may reflect tensions within the messianist movement over the status of the Law and the Gentile mission,[6] and Luke's depiction of the Pharisees closing ranks with Paul against the Sadducees on the question of the resurrection (Acts 23:6-10) must be taken seriously as a glimpse of the tensions among authorities, institutions, and groups over Israel's identity and role in God's design for the world.

It is at least clear that Luke-Acts manifests a struggle among the messianists as part of a complex of disputes among various Jewish groups over how to be "true Israel," what the sins which call for repentance may be, and what role the Gentiles have to play in God's judgment and salvation. It is also clear that it is no longer credible to disregard the complexity of late first-century Jewish history by reading Luke-Acts simply as a story of "Christianity" versus "Judaism." Those terms may acquire their meaning only in the social and religious context of subsequent centuries.

The narrative of Luke-Acts is not a straightforward account of the triumph of "Christian history" nor of the ascendancy of Gentile Christianity out of the ashes of Jewish history. The theme of the rejection of the Messiah and of the preaching of the apostles has been shown to be a major "plot device" of the whole story, filling the narrative with genuine pathos and tragedy and urgency.[7] The unity of the narrative requires that Luke 1–2 be read in relation to Acts 28. Both the hopeful promises and the painful words of judgment are not only filled with prophetic precedent, but these declarations and oracles alert the reader that the fundamental tension of the plot still awaits a final resolution. The struggle of wills between a determined God and a willful Israel remains intense, awaiting the repentance which must still precede the restoration of all in the kingdom of the exalted Messiah (see Acts 3:19; 1:8; 28:23-28).[8]

II. THE STORY OF THE FALL AND RISE OF MANY IN ISRAEL

Before the literary complexity of Luke-Acts could be explored, the unity of the narrative had to be grasped anew. Henry J. Cadbury's monumental assessment, *The Making of Luke-Acts,*[9] still stands like a beacon on the far side of the tireless labors of the source and redaction critics of the 1930s to the 1960s. Remarkably, many of the very materials which the source critics were so eager to assign to earlier "Jewish" stages of the tradition have emerged again as fundamental to Luke's literary project. The coherence and significance of the speeches in Acts and the infancy narratives are particularly telling cases. Through whatever traditions or sources these stories and their declarations may have been conveyed to the author, they are now Lukan compositions, and those who speak within these passages are reliable narrators.[10]

The oracles of Simeon are thus captured in a larger presentation of the circumcision of the Messiah and his portentous presentation in the temple in Luke 2. The thorough structuring of the annunciation, birth, and childhood stories is so prominent as to invite close comparison of these wonder children throughout their ensuing careers[11] (see also Luke 7:16-19, 26-35; 16:16; Acts 10:37-38). But the angels, faithful elders of Israel, and mother of the infant Messiah, who give voice to the canticles and oracles concerning these children, are all to be implicitly trusted. This includes Zechariah, who is struck dumb for rather mild disbelief but later prophesies as one filled with the Holy Spirit (Luke 1:20,67-79). The literary function of these episodes is, therefore, to sound the critical themes of the story in advance of the telling. They declare the promises and perils which God's rule will bring to bear on Israel and the nations through this Messiah and his herald, John. The speeches in Acts, in turn, serve to identify the ways this purpose and plan of God has unfolded (see especially Acts 2:14-36; 3:12-26; 4:24-30; 10:34-43).

The general tone of these prophetic declarations in Luke 1–2 is joyful, full of hope and confidence, and extravagant in their vision of God's reign. John will precede Jesus "in the spirit and power of Elijah, to turn the hearts of the fathers to the children, and the disobedient to the wisdom of the just, to make ready for the Lord a people prepared" (1:17). This is the way in which God has "visited and redeemed his people," saving them from the fear of their enemies, guiding their feet in the way of peace (1:68-79). Jesus will be given the throne of his father David, "and of his kingdom there will be no end." This is how God has "put down the mighty from their thrones and exalted those of low degree" (1:51-55). The reader is thus not surprised at the political connection that this birth took place within the census of Caesar Augustus during Quirinius's governance of Syria. When the heavenly messenger declares, "To you is born this day in the city of David a Savior, who is Christ the Lord," it is clear that Jesus' messiahship has everything to do with Israel's fate within the Roman order.

But, as Robert Tannehill has shown so clearly,[12] all of this optimism and hopefulness is poignant and potentially tragic in Luke's narrative. First, the retrospective sermons, culminating in the last word of Acts 28, are not accounts of the gathering of all faithful Israel with the triumph of the Messiah over Israel's enemies, but rather the recitation by the exalted Messiah's apostle and witness of Isaiah's indictment of Israel's deafness, blindness, and hardness of heart. Second, if Jerusalem and the temple had already been destroyed by the time Luke wrote this narrative, the promise which the Messiah first portended for Israel could now be merely a bitter reminder of failed hopes or recriminations for lack of repentance. Certainly the sense of an ending which could be derived from Acts 28 is that the recitation of God's salvation history points only to the condemnation of Israel.

It must be granted that this view of the narrative as an indictment has literary probability. Stephen's speech in Acts 7 testifies that the salvation history which God intends may again be the damnation history of a "stiff-necked people, uncircumcised in heart and ears, always resisting the Holy Spirit" (7:51). Furthermore, there is nothing anti-Jewish or foreign to Jewish tradition in such indictment. The prophetic heritage long before taught how Israel's history could be recited against her. The book of Deuteronomy is even constructed with such a sense of an ending in which Moses' speech, uttered before the fact, announces destruction which verges on the utter annihilation of Israel (Deuteronomy 31–34). Jewish literature of the era surrounding the destruction of the second temple is replete with such strong prophetic diagnoses. Israel has always known how to confess sin, and Luke's narrative is a call to Israel to repent by accepting Jesus as Messiah and not "withstanding God" (see Acts 2:37-38; 3:19; 5:31; 17:30; 26:20).

It is also possible that Luke's narrative is fundamentally a tragic tale in which the hopeful promises which have been so joyfully announced are now only intensifications of their failure. Certainly, like many of his contemporary historians, Luke knew many of the conventions of tragic historiography. His version of the death of Jesus is particularly marked with such pathos and remorse and the haunting double vision of those who go blindly to their destruction.[13] The effect of such narratives must be assessed with extreme care, however, since tragic style may only be veiled self-justification, as when Josephus adopts the tragic mode to exonerate himself and the Romans or when Melito of Sardis stirs up hatred against the Jews while posturing deep sympathy.[14]

It seems more likely that Luke's hopeful assurances in the infancy stories are to be taken at face value. They are not oracles doomed

25

to fail. The harsh prophetic words and laments of the Messiah and his apostles still stand in sharp contrast, indicating that the course of the fulfillment of these promises has not been easy or direct. The tragic proportions and potential of the story are such that the readers are profoundly aware that even God's saving will for Israel and the Gentiles is threatened. As Paul Minear has shown, even Luke's presentation of the "boldness" and "confidence" of the apostles is probably symptomatic of an "internal dialogue between credulity and skepticism" in a community where the possibility of failed hopes must be addressed.[15]

These hopes are consistently stated in terms of God's promises to Israel. The persons who have the hopes and the content of their expectations are constantly identified in the language of the scriptural promises to Israel. Consider Luke's cardinal expressions of this yearning: Simeon, who was "looking for the consolation of Israel" (Luke 2:25); Anna, the prophetess, daughter of Phanuel, worshiping day and night and giving thanks to God and speaking of Jesus "to all who were looking for the redemption of Jerusalem" (2:38); Joseph, of the Jewish town of Arimathea, "a good and righteous man, who had not consented to their purpose and deed, and . . . was looking for the kingdom of God" (23:50-51); Cleopas and his companion, who "had hoped that he was the one to redeem Israel" (24:21); Jesus' own disciples, who asked, "Lord will you at this time restore the kingdom to Israel?" (Acts 1:8, see also Luke 19:11); James, looking forward to the fulfillment of the prophetic promise of the rebuilding of "the dwelling of David which has fallen" (Acts 15:16); and Paul, who emphasized that it was for his "hope in the promise made by God to our fathers" that he was on trial (Acts 26:6, see also 24:15; 26:23). If Luke's stated purpose for his narrative is that the reader "may know the truth concerning the things of which you have been informed" (Luke 1:1-4), it is inconceivable that the hopes of these faithful in Israel will finally be disappointed.

Simeon's oracles, therefore, are crucial to the meaning of the narrative as a whole, because Simeon announces Israel's hope as God's will in no uncertain terms, but he also alerts the reader that Jesus will provoke a crisis in Israel. His own credentials are above reproach, and the repeated mention of the Holy Spirit confirms all that he expects to see and does see. "This man was righteous and devout, looking for the consolation of Israel, and the Holy Spirit was upon him" (Luke 2:25; see also 2:26, "It had been revealed to him by the Holy Spirit," and 2:27, "And inspired by the Spirit he came into the temple"). Jesus, Mary and Joseph, and Simeon are all fully obedient and observant of all dimensions of the Law of Moses (2:21-23, so also Anna, 2:37).[16] Simeon's two oracles foreshadow the entire story, providing a portentous glimpse of what the Holy Spirit had long said through the prophets and would continue to say (see also Acts 28:25) concerning the purposes of God and the prospects of Israel.

The first oracle announces what the infant Messiah means to God. It is a testimony given in the form of Simeon's blessing of God, declaring the faithfulness of God to the word given to Simeon and to the scriptural promises which it echoes. The parallelism of the passage indicates that the "salvation which thou hast prepared in the face of all the peoples" is the same as "the light" which is given "for revelation to the Gentiles" and "for the glory of your people Israel." Even on a strictly literal level, the passage identifies God's salvation as a public disclosure in view of all the Gentiles but redounding to Israel's glory. The possibility that some of the Gentiles could see the light before all of Israel is gathered has already been broached, yet without any hint of rebuke of Israel. This first inspired oracle has disclosed that God's purposes and plans are wholly directed toward salvation. When seen in connection with Simeon's expectation of the "consolation of Israel," this "salvation" has the clear connotation of the "redemption," "restoration," "kingdom," and "hope" which all of the other worthies in the story await.

But as Jesus' "father and mother" are amazed and filled with wonder at this first oracle, Simeon speaks a second oracle, which seems to confound the first or threaten it with tragedy. Uttered now as a "blessing" of Jesus' human parents and as a word to Mary, Simeon's oracle alerts the reader to the complexity of God's way of accomplishing the saving reign of this Messiah. Certainly Simeon is still inspired and speaking for God, but now he is advising the reader along with the faithful Mary and Joseph that even God's salvation in Jesus will bring down many in Israel before it will have accomplished God's ultimate gracious purpose.[17] Humanity, and Israel and Mary in particular, are put on notice that God's reign or visitation of Israel is a divine confrontation with a willful people as well as a consolation to the faithful (see Luke 1:68-69; 19:44). This salvation will be accomplished by God, but it will also produce human suffering (see also Acts 9:16). The sequence of words is significant. This is not a prediction of the rise and fall of the Roman Empire, the Third Reich, or the kingdom of Herod. This is a prophetic oracle disclosing the fall which will come before the rising of many in Israel, and the passive voice alerts the reader once again that it is God who has set this child for such falling and rising and for being a controverted sign. This is the reader's advance warning of the way in which even unwilling human agents in the story would be found doing "whatever God's hand and will had predetermined would take place" (Acts 3:28). And God's initiative in this confrontation had the purpose ("in order that") of exposing the "secret thoughts *(dialogismoi)* of the hearts of many" (Luke 2:35). These are the veiled rejections (Luke 4:22; 5:22; 6:8; 13:31; 19:39), the misguided illusions (Luke 9:9, 46-47; 23:8), and doubts (Luke 24:38) which Jesus exposes in his adversaries and his disciples alike.

The "many in Israel" who will fall and rise in order that their rejection or resistance to God's reign be exposed will continue to be in the center of the narrative of Luke-Acts, with only a few episodes of similar rejections by Samaritans or Gentiles. This will be a story of a struggle of wills with a Messiah who will confront the people in Nazareth (Luke 4:16-30), "some Pharisees" who attempt to divert Jesus from his way to Jerusalem (Luke 13:34; 19:39-40), and those who send spies, "pretending to be sincere" but in reality are intent on trapping the Messiah (Luke 20:20). So also the apostles who call Israel to repentance will constantly encounter resistance and rejection throughout the entire story of Acts. Even the threefold turning to the Gentiles, which punctuates Paul's mission in Acts (13:46; 18:6; 28:28), is always involved with the fall and rise of many in Israel. The last word is always about Israel, not only in Acts 28 but even in the Lord's word to Ananias concerning Paul: "He is a chosen instrument of mine to carry my name before the Gentiles and kings and the sons of Israel" (Acts 9:15). Far from concluding that God or the Messiah or the apostles are done with Israel, the whole of the narrative rather demonstrates that even the Gentile mission is fundamental to God's determination to deal with a willful Israel. But the salvation which God intends, the restoration of all, and the kingdom of God itself are to be attested to Israel at the beginning and at the end.

The ending of the narrative in Acts 28 is, therefore, not the end of the story, but it is a resumption of the themes sounded in Simeon's oracles. First, Paul lays claim to his credentials as a faithful Israelite (Acts 28:17), while acknowledging that he remains in bonds because the "Judeans" had "spoken against" him.[18] Paul is asked to speak on behalf of "this sect which is everywhere spoken against" (Acts 28:22). Since Jesus has been identified as a "sign spoken against" (Luke 2:34), the reader ought not be surprised to find that the messianist sect *(hairesis)* and its apostle would share that fate. Similarly the "great numbers" (Acts 28:23) of those who come and largely reject Paul's testimony are at least reminiscent of the "many" in Israel who were predicted to "fall and rise" and whose "secret thoughts of the heart" were to be disclosed.

Now again Paul discerns, as Simeon did, that the Holy Spirit is speaking in the words of the prophet Isaiah to disclose "the hearts of this people." Like Simeon, Paul speaks to the end about salvation by testifying to the kingdom of God and the Messiah and Lord Jesus (Acts 28:23,31). Both of Simeon's oracles are still valid guides for grasping the scene, now as augmented by Paul's quote of Isaiah. God is determined that this salvation and reign of Jesus be for light to the Gentiles and unto the glory of Israel, but for the present the hearts of many in Israel have been disclosed to be hardened against the understanding and healing which God intends for Israel.

III. THE GENTILE QUESTION

Within the literary structure of the narrative, a scriptural argument is also pursued which provides another level of insight into what is at stake in the story. In fact, Luke-Acts provides a response to a cluster of related questions, which persist from Luke 1–2 to Acts 28 and are anchored in the Christian claim that the Scriptures have been fulfilled and the Holy Spirit, the "promise of the Father," has been given. Have the promises which God made to Israel failed? Have the prophetic oracles only become an indictment with power merely to condemn and not to save Israel? If the Messiah has come, why has not all of Israel been gathered, restored, forgiven, consoled, and redeemed? And how can the mission among the Gentiles be justified, especially the Pauline mission which is vulnerable to criticism for its aggressive initiatives beyond Israel and for the inclusion of Gentiles without their complete observance of the Torah?

First-century Israel knew about the "light for revelation to the Gentiles." They had read and pondered the Isaiah passages: "I have given you as a covenant to the people, a light to the nations . . ." (Isa. 42:6); "It is too light a thing that you should be my servant to raise up the tribes of Jacob and to restore the preserved of Israel; I will give you as a light to the nations that my salvation may reach the end of the earth" (Isa. 49:6). This was the vocation of the servant of God and of Israel. But how was this vocation to be exercised? How were these passages to be construed?

Israel also knew the peril of going the way of the Gentiles and their idols and abandoning faithfulness to the Law of Moses. Deuteronomy and the prophets were full of such warnings, declaring that God would then use the Gentiles as the instrument of divine vengeance. The book of Jubilees begins its recitation of history as indictment and call for repentance by stressing that Israel will abandon the Law. "They will forget all my commandments that I have given them and copy the Gentiles, their uncleanness and their shame, and worship their gods; and these will prove a stumbling-block to them, a source of distress and misery, and a snare" (Jub. 1:9). Then God will "hand them over to the Gentiles to be taken captive and to be preyed upon and to be devoured" (1:14). Only "after this they will turn to me from among the Gentiles with all their heart and with all their soul and with all their strength . . . and they shall be a blessing and not a curse" (1:16-17; see Gen. 22:18). "And I will circumcise the foreskin of their heart and the foreskin of the heart of their sons, and I will create in them a holy spirit, and I will cleanse them so that they shall not turn away from me again, from that day until eternity" (Jub. 1:10-11). Repentance is the theme, and Israel's relationship to the Gentiles is the focal issue. Restoration, and cleansing of the heart, and the presence of a holy spirit— all are at stake. But Jubilees is most concerned with the danger of those who would "teach all the Jews who are among the Gentiles to forsake Moses, telling them not to circumcise their children or observe the customs" (to use the words of Acts 21:21; see also 15:1).[19]

Second Baruch and 4 Ezra, non-Christian documents contemporary with Acts, also ponder Israel's suffering after the Roman destruction of Jerusalem in terms of the place of the Gentiles in God's economy. Neither document could conceive of any salvation of the Gentiles apart from the observance of the Torah. Nevertheless, 4 Ezra does envision the gathering of a people from among the Gentiles ahead of Israel as a reproach and a call for repentance: "When I came to them they rejected me and refused the Lord's commandment. Therefore I say to you, O nations that hear and understand, 'Await your shepherd; he will give you everlasting rest, because he who will come at the end of the age is close at hand. Be ready for the rewards of the kingdom, because the eternal light will shine on you forevermore'" (4 Ezra 2:33-35; see also 2:10; 4:23, "Israel has been given over to the Gentiles as a reproach").[20]

Second Baruch shares the conviction that the present is a time of judgment of Israel and that the Gentiles are God's instruments, but the last word will still be the fulfillment of God's promises: "Let us not now fix our attention upon the delights the Gentiles enjoy in the present age, but let us remember what has been promised to us in the end" (2 Bar. 83:5). Even the present time may be of some benefit to the Gentiles, and Israel's mission must not be neglected. In the face of Israel's sin, God said, "I will scatter this people among the Gentiles, that they may do good to the Gentiles" (1:4); and "then after a short interval, Zion will be rebuilt, and its offerings will be restored again, and the priests will return to their ministry, and the Gentiles will come and acclaim it" (68:5).[21]

The Jewish-Christian "Testaments of the Twelve Patriarchs" displays how this discussion of Israel's relationship to the Gentiles continued into the second century. The scriptural traditions have been mediated to this author through a heritage of Jewish postbiblical interpretations.[22] But now the salvation of the Gentiles is fundamental to Israel's own fulfillment. Thus another Simeon testifies concerning Levi and Judah: "It is from them that God's salvation will come to you. For the Lord will raise up from Levi as it were a high priest, and from Judah as it were a king, God and man: he will save all Gentiles and the race of Israel" (T. Simeon 7:1-2). And Levi offers another paraphrase of Isaiah's verses concerning Israel as the "light to the nations": "A bright light of knowledge will make you shine in Jacob, and like the sun you will be to the whole race of Israel. And a blessing shall be given to you and all your sons, until the Lord looks upon all the Gentiles with the affection of his son for ever" (T. Levi 4:3-4).[23]

Luke's version of the oracles of Simeon clearly belongs within this larger Jewish discussion of Israel's place among the nations within God's design and election. This was never a merely theoretical discussion, since Israel's identity and divine vocation were at stake, but the deliberation and debate became especially intense and difficult in the wake of the Roman destruction of Jerusalem and the temple. Not only was this a national calamity; but according to Israel's Scriptures, this was a reenactment of divine judgment on sinful Israel.

None of the literary testimonies cited above stated directly that Jerusalem had been ravaged by Rome. They were all composed as prophetic words after the fact, whether in the form of ancient utterances concerning the first destruction or as the oracles of an aged worthy seer who, having been blessed to "see the Lord's Messiah" (Luke 2:26), offered a prognosis of what the appearance of this "salvation" would mean to Israel and the Gentiles. None of them stated explicitly what their story proved about the pressing questions of their own day nor identified the intended audience of the work in any complete way. Perhaps these narratives survived in part because they did not foreclose the profound questions too quickly. Why have things turned out this way? What is the sin which requires repentance? What hope is there? Nevertheless, each narrative is a testimony of what it all means, a theodicy interpreting God's ways with Israel and the world, and a call for repentance leading to restoration.[24]

It would be helpful to the interpretation of Luke-Acts to know a great deal more about the occasion and context of its production. Both a literary analysis and an examination of the scriptural exposition of the narrative demonstrate the thoroughly Jewish (or Israelite) character of the story, and even the prominence of the justification of the Gentile mission leaves many convictions about God and Israel unstated, or only implied. Is this a Gentile author and community now reaching back to lay claim to Israel's heritage, or a Jewish-Christian movement staking out the ground of "true Israel," or a mixed community of Jewish and Gentile Christians responding to a persistently powerful minority of strictly observant Jewish Christians?[25] In any case, the oracles of Simeon demonstrate that the question of the status of the Gentiles is fundamental to Luke's view of God's relationship to Israel.

But Luke has no romantic view of the Gentiles, no notion of a progressive history where the favor the gods once displayed toward the Greeks has now been transferred to the Romans. The success of the Gentile mission is a reproach to Israel, and even Paul, God's "chosen instrument" of this mission, is thus still dealing with Israel. Deuteronomy and the prophets and the intertestamental traditions expressed all kinds of divine threats toward Israel and saw God's blessing of the Gentiles as a reproach toward Israel, but they never entertained the idea that God would ever be faithless, even to a faithless people. Furthermore, the Gentiles are still understood by Luke to be the means of divine vengeance, but these are not Gentile Christians. When Luke speaks of Jerusalem being "trodden down by the Gentiles, until the times of the Gentiles are fulfilled" (Luke 21:24), the message is as clear as in 4 Ezra or 2 Baruch that the times of Gentile domination of Israel will be limited by God's own righteousness. God's vengeance and vindication have their times of wrath and restoration, and the Messiah has already been exalted to God's right hand as "Leader and Savior in order to give repentance to Israel and forgiveness of sins" (Acts 5:31).

Then the mission of repentant Israel, of faithful Israel, is also to be a "light to the Gentiles." It is God who has given this repentance "even" to the Gentiles (Acts 11:18), and neither the apostles nor Israel can "withstand God" (11:17; see also Gamaliel's counsel in 5:39). This calling may become a reproach to those who reject the "word of God" (13:46-47), but it is Israel's vocation and blessing. The "glory of thy people Israel" is to be the "light for the revelation to the Gentiles." Just as 2 Baruch suggested that even in the time of Gentile triumph God wanted Israel to "do good to the Gentiles" (2 Bar. 1:4), so Luke-Acts affirms the legitimacy of the Gentile mission without ever suggesting that Gentile supremacy is the final will of God.

God is never done with Israel in any of the scriptural, intertestamental, or New Testament documents, and Luke-Acts is no exception. God may be contending with Israel, even causing Israel to stumble, bringing "many in Israel" low in order that the salvation which God intends may be brought through repentance and restoration. Although in subsequent eras the narrative of Luke-Acts would be read only at Israel's expense or with a sympathetic regard for a failed history, it was and remains a story of God's determined purpose to redeem Israel and even to restore Israel's glory of bringing the light of God's reign to the Gentiles. At the center of the story, God's resurrection and exaltation of Jesus is God's way of finally transcending the tragic rejection of the Messiah and its real consequences for Jerusalem. Simeon's dire oracle concerning the falling of many in Israel and a sign spoken against has already been amply fulfilled within the narrative and at its end (Acts 28) and probably in Luke's world. But the restoration, the consolation, the redemption, the repentance, the forgiveness, and the reign of God which Simeon and all those other worthies in Israel expected has only begun to be inaugurated in the present time of Luke's story.

3

THE IRONIC FULFILLMENT
OF ISRAEL'S GLORY

David P. Moessner

D avid Tiede's primary assertion is that when the hopeful promises of Luke 1 and 2 are compared with the somber warnings against Israel at the conclusion of Acts, it becomes clear that "the fundamental tension of the plot still awaits a final resolution." [1] As he develops this thesis in three parts, it also becomes manifest in his discussion of the Simeon oracle in part II [2] that he could just as well have said, "the fundamental tension of the plot still awaits *its decisive* resolution." For in articulating his subthesis, that "Simeon's two oracles foreshadow the entire story, providing a portentous glimpse of . . . the purposes of God and the prospects of Israel," [3] Tiede interprets the "falling of many" to refer essentially to the story of the two-volume Luke-Acts, while the "rising of many in Israel" remains the fundamental promise standing open, waiting to be fulfilled. Accordingly Tiede concludes at the very end, "Simeon's dire oracle . . . has already been amply fulfilled within the narrative. . . . But the restoration, the consolation, the redemption, the repentance, the forgiveness, and the reign of God which Simeon and all those other worthies in Israel expected has only begun to be inaugurated in the present time of Luke's story." [4]

Before assessing this thesis and proposing an alternative rendering of this "tension," it will be helpful first to trace the logic of Tiede's main points in parts II and III of his chapter.

Careful literary-critical studies in recent years have demonstrated not only the complexity of the various parts but also the overarching unity that Luke has fashioned from these parts in his two volumes.

Especially significant are the infancy stories of Luke 1–2, which have been carefully structured in order to "sound the critical themes of the story in advance of the telling."[5] At the heart of these themes are the optimistic, joyful promises of the final fulfillment of God's reign in a Messiah and Savior through whom Israel is redeemed from her enemies as the "mighty" are "put down from their thrones." But alas, as the story progresses, particularly in the Acts, it becomes obvious that these promises are far from describing Israel's actual predicament within the Roman world. Especially if the temple and Jerusalem have already been destroyed when Luke writes, the glowing hopes of Luke 1 and 2 would all the more be cruel reminders of God's punishment rather than salvation to Israel. Tiede agrees with Robert Tannehill that reading the promises of the beginning in light of the end of Acts could lead to a sense of tragic proportions for the story of Israel.[6] "Certainly the sense of an ending which could be derived from Acts 28 is that the recitation of God's salvation history points only to the condemnation of Israel."[7]

Here then is Tiede's problematic. The promises of final salvation, uttered through such pious, reliable witnesses of Luke 1 and 2, seem finally to be shattered at the end. But have the promises of God failed?[8] Tiede resounds with an emphatic no!

a. Simeon's second oracle of "falling and rising" and a "controverted sign" (Luke 2:34b-35) is the reader's "advance warning"[9] that God's salvation will come only through a thoroughgoing confrontation with a willful, disobedient people. Great suffering will be the means of the falling of many *before* many "rise" in the final gathering of God's reign.

b. The course of the story itself testifies to the programmatic character of Simeon's second oracle. All through Acts Messiah's chosen witnesses confront an obstinate Israel, with the result that the dynamic of "falling and rising" continues through the very end of Acts 28. "The ending of the narrative in Acts 28 is, therefore, not the end of the story, but it is a resumption of the themes sounded in Simeon's oracles."[10]

c. Israel's rejection or "falling" is part and parcel of a scriptural argument throughout Luke-Acts that attempts to answer how the church can maintain that the Scriptures, including the promise of the Holy Spirit, are fulfilled precisely in the midst of Israel's refusal but at the same time in the Gentile's acceptance of Israel's messianic salvation. The servant of Isaiah's pattern of vocation constitutes the crux of the argument. As also reflected in various Jewish intertestamental writings—Tiede cites Jubilees, 2 Baruch, 4 Ezra, and the Testaments of the Twelve Patriarchs—Gentile nations serve as the instruments of God's punishment for Israel's rejection, as in Luke 21:21-24. But, in one way or another, Israel's interaction with the Gentiles brings these nations the blessing of the light of revelation even as it points forward to Israel's ultimate gathering and restoration in God's final salvation. What is significant for Luke-Acts, Tiede avers, is that the Gentile mission carried out by a repenting, faithful Israel, while bringing reproach to Israel, nevertheless spells promise and hope and final inclusion for *un*believing Israel in the salvific purposes of God. For, in extending the messianic salvation to the nations, Israel is fulfilling its own glory as the "light of revelation," a "glory"/task which unfailingly illuminates the truth in all of the scriptural, intertestamental, and New Testament documents that "God is never done with Israel."[11]

In this and other works Tiede has convincingly shown that the "heartbeat" of Luke's two volumes is the story of Israel or, as he himself says, "The last word is always about Israel."[12] For these insights Lukan scholarship is greatly in his debt. Yet, in light of the story that Luke actually presents, the way Tiede has formulated the problematic and, consequently, the place where the emphasis falls are surprising indeed.

THE PRIMARY TENSION OF THE PLOT

Can it possibly be true that Luke intends his readers to take all the promises of Luke 1–2 "at face value"?[13] To be sure, in this immediate context Tiede means that the "hopeful assurances" are to be taken "seriously" as promises that *will be fulfilled*. With this I could not agree more fully. Yet, as one continues through parts II and III, it becomes evident that Tiede is setting all the concrete hopes and images of coming salvation in Luke 1–2 on a par under a common rubric, i.e., "promises," and that by "face value" Tiede means "literally." Thus, for instance, when Mary, a reliable witness to God's intentions, declares that God "has [will] put down the mighty from their thrones and exalted those of humble status" (1:52), we are to take the *primary* referent literally; so at the end of Acts when Caesar and the Roman governors are still firmly in control and the messianic movement is "everywhere spoken against," it is excruciatingly obvious that this "hopeful assurance" is anything but fulfilled! Or if an Anna or a Zechariah—again both endowed by the narrator with the characteristics of trustworthy spokespersons—speak of "Jerusalem's redemption" or of "deliverance from the fear of our enemies," and Luke's readers have experienced or know of the Roman destruction of the temple and city, then, as Tiede says, "the *promise*[!]"[14] which the Messiah first portended for Israel could now be merely a bitter reminder of failed hopes or recriminations for lack of repentance."[15] Here again we are to understand Luke's intended *primary* referent within his two-volume story-world as literal. Hence the great discrepancy between promise and fulfillment, "the fundamental tension of the plot" that "still awaits a final resolution."[16] As we have seen, Tiede's solution is to point to Simeon's oracles as the focusing lens for both Luke 1 and 2, so that the readers know that first Israel must "fall" *before* the promise(s) of their salvation is (are) realized.

But surely our narrator would have us understand the tension in a fundamentally different way. The tension, I would submit, is ironic. That is to say, what certain characters believe and express as a hope or promise on one level is meant to be perceived by the readers on a different level. Thus when Simeon, who is looking for the "consolation" of Israel (a Deutero-Isaiah term),[17] declares that this child is the fulfillment of the "saving act" of God *(sotērion)* of the Isaianic promises precisely through the servant's mission of rejection and the dividing of Israel, are we not at least to wonder whether Mary's and Zechariah's bold declarations of defeat are to be understood perhaps in a different vein? Is Simeon's word essentially only a *temporal* qualifier for the other expectations? Moreover, we can already observe that neither angelic announcement mentions a nationalistic or militaristic kingdom with defeat of enemies: John will prepare a people of repentance through the power of Holy Spirit (1:13-17), and Jesus will reign on the throne of David forever (1:31-33); but again any immediate clues as to how this will take place mention *only* the power of Holy Spirit (1:34-38). On a prima facie level, then, the *only* justification for interpreting the "divine" revealer, Gabriel, necessarily in a literal nationalistic sense is to dovetail and substantively equate these revelations with the pronouncements of Mary and Zechariah, as Tiede (and Tannehill) have done.

But that this is not what our narrator wants us to do becomes manifest as the story progresses through Luke's creation of a dramatic tension between the expectations of pious Israel and what the plan *(boulē)* of God will actually effect. In order to measure the pulse of this discrepancy it will be helpful to utilize "point of view" and "omniscient" narration, especially as the latter is defined by Meir Sternberg in his *The Poetics of Biblical Narrative*.[18] The omniscient mode

> manifests all the privileges of knowledge that transcend the human condition. For one thing the narrator has free access to the minds ("hearts") of the dramatis personae, not excluding God himself. . . . For another, he enjoys free movement in time (among narrative past, present, and future) and in space (enabling him to follow secret conversations, shuttle between simultaneous happenings or between heaven and earth). These two establish an unlimited range of information to draw upon or, from the reader's side, a supernatural principle of coherence and intelligibility. For the narrative provides us with an assortment of plot-stuff that would normally be inaccessible.[19]

From 1:5 "Luke" (cf. 1:1-4) slips behind the narrator and quickly establishes the mode of narration as omniscient,[20] as the narrator freely moves his readers "from above" from one locale to another (e.g., from the temple to the hill country of Judea, 1:24; to Galilee, 1:26), reveals angelic pronouncements in heavenly visitations (e.g., 1:11-23, 26-38), "quotes" private thoughts and desires (e.g., 1:25; 2:19), and cites prophetic interpretations of "interior" and supraterrestrial events (e.g., 1:41-45, 46-55, 67-79). This third person mode is sustained to the end, 24:53, in the course of which the narrator presents God's voice directly (e.g., 3:22b; 9:35), interprets the "word of God" as a direct spokesman for God (e.g., 3:2→3:4-6), and declares how the disciples misunderstood God's intention in the words of Jesus (e.g., 9:45; 18:34). Clearly he aligns his omniscient vantage point with God's own omniscient perspective.

But which of the characters within the story speaks for God? In light of Tiede's portrayal of Luke 1–2, the question we are most interested in is whether our narrator fuses his own (and God's) point of view more closely to one or more of the *dramatis personae,* or whether all inspired figures speak "equally" or representatively for him (and God). Jesus, of course, is a likely candidate (see below) and presumably angelic host, like Gabriel "the angel/messenger of the Lord" (1:11,19a), speak directly for God, especially since the narrator has Gabriel say to Zechariah, "I . . . who stand in the presence of God and have been *sent* to speak to you and to proclaim *(euangelisasthai)* these things to you" (1:19b; cf. 2:10), And yet, as many have noted, our narrator would also seem to endow the human characters Zechariah, Mary, Elizabeth, and, later, Simeon and Anna with inspired, authoritative speech: e. g., "filled/overcome with Holy Spirit" (1:35,41,67; 2:25-27); "prophesying" or "prophetess" (1:67,68-79; 2:36); interpreting spontaneously and in ecstatic speech the fulfillment of the word of the Lord through Gabriel (1:42-45) and "the fathers" (1:46-54,68-79). But do all these speak equally for God? For instance, when Mary (1:47-55) or Zechariah (1:69-79) speaks of Israel's enemies, are they the Lord God's/the narrator's enemies or main antagonists that will be presented in the ensuing story?

The scope of this essay does not permit a detailed analysis of point of view in Luke-Acts or even a thorough tracing of the tensions between promise and fulfillment. After arguing that Simeon and Anna are depicted as special spokespersons for the omniscient point of view in a way that not only temporally qualifies but also qualitatively redefines the passel of prophetic hopes and expectations in Luke 1, we must be content to snatch a few glimpses at strategic points in the rest of the plot that confirm this role for Simeon and Anna.

1. The narrator limits significantly the knowledge/understanding that Zechariah, Mary, and Elizabeth possess of the divine plan announced by Gabriel and then by the angelic host (Luke 2:10-14) and thus *limits* their ability to speak for God (and the narrator). In contrast, Simeon and Anna are not so delimited. *(a)* Wonder and mystery enshroud the recipients of the angelophanies. There is great "fear" (Zechariah, 1:12-13; Mary, 1:50; shepherds, 2:9-10; cf. Judean residents, 1:65) or "consternation" (Zechariah, 1:12; Mary, 1:29), and a great mystique or "awesomeness" that defies normal categories of human experience and requires a "laying or pondering or storing of these things in [the] heart" (Mary, 2:19; cf. 2:51; Elizabeth goes into "retreat," 1:24; cf. the Judean hill country residents, 1:66). It is interesting that Mary's (and Joseph's) response of "wonder" to Simeon's oracle (2:33) is characterized in the same way as that of the *laos* outside the sanctuary, 1:21, and that of the

Judean country folk, 1:63; 2:18. *(b)* Our narrator spares no effort to discredit Zechariah's credentials as an omniscient spokesman as this first great "worthy" of the story is struck *dumb* by Gabriel for "unbelief" (1:20). *(c)* Special credentials are given to Simeon:[21] (i) He has received a specific revelation (*kechrēmatismenon*, 2:26), a "word" (*rhēma*, 2:29b) of the Lord (cf. 3:2) "by the Holy Spirit." (ii) He is guided "by (in) the Spirit" (cf. 4:1,14) to the temple precisely when the "word" is to be fulfilled. (iii) He "blesses" Mary,[22] the recipient of a "word" "from God" (1:37-38) and the "mother of the Lord" (1:43). (iv) Most importantly, Simeon, like Gabriel, reveals to Mary what her child will be in God's intent (e.g., *keitai*, 2:34) for salvation and even what her own role will be (2:30-34, 35; cf. 1:28-33, 35-37). But now the plot narrows suddenly and substantially. This one who will be called "Yahweh saves" (1:31, Gabriel) and "Savior" (2:11, angel of the Lord) is God's "saving act" (*sotērion*, Simeon) precisely as a "controverted sign" who causes the "falling and rising of *many* [2:34b] in Israel" (2:30, 34). This one who will be called "Son of God" or "Son of the Most High" and "reign as king upon the throne of David forever" (1:32-33), and as the "anointed one" bring "peace" to "folk of God's gracious favor" (2:11, 14), will reign as the "anointed of the Lord" (2:26) and bring "peace" (2:29) precisely as that "sword of discernment"[23] which pierces the very "heart" of the "*many* [2:35b] in Israel," even including the "mother of the Lord" (2:35; cf. 1:43). *(d)* Anna confirms Simeon's revelation to those like Mary and Zechariah who are awaiting or expecting liberation for Jerusalem (2:38; cf. 24:21!). In chiastic sequence she thus offsets and redefines the literal nationalistic-political messianic expectations of Mary (cf. 1:46-55), as Simeon does for Zechariah's hopes (cf. 1:68-79). When the narrator closes the closely intersecting panels of the births and childhoods of John and Jesus with Mary again "wondering in amazement" (2:48,50; cf. 2:33) and her expectations for Jesus and his "father's" "son" suspended in incredulity in the affairs of his "Father" (2:48b-49→2:51b), we the readers ourselves may wonder whether God's saving act will indeed match the hopes of pious Israel.

2. In the opening description of John's public preaching to Israel (Luke 3:1-6), our narrator continues to narrow the characteristic features and plot that will swirl about Jesus and God's salvation as

he narrows the parameters of John's calling as well: *(a)* After summing up John's ministry in Luke 3:3 as the "proclaiming of a baptism of repentance leading to the release of sins," the narrator, by quoting Isa. 40:3-5, declares directly what the significance of the "word of God" to John in the wilderness (Luke 3:2) is all about and precisely with respect to this "proclaiming. . ." (3:3). As Gabriel had already declared, John has a special calling to *prepare* a repentant people as he goes "before the Lord" (1:16-17); but John goes "before the Lord" as the "voice" or "herald" of the Deutero-Isaianic salvation who must *prepare* the way so that "all flesh" may see the "saving act of God" (*sotērion*, 3:6→2:30; cf. "*prepared* before the face of all peoples," 2:31). Hence, speaking omnisciently, our narrator dovetails John's role into the Isaianic prophecies of Simeon and Anna. *(b)* This funneling of John's role is substantiated as John's preaching of the "mightier one," "the anointed one" who is coming with eschatological judgment of fire (3:15-17), is radically reoriented. That John is voicing expectations similar to those of Mary or Zechariah of a Messiah who will destroy the enemies of God's salvation is clear in 3:17. The "fire" of 3:16 is the fire of destruction that "burns up the chaff." And already the axe of judgment is "laid to the root" of dead wood, as John demands specific deeds "worthy of repentance" (3:7-14). Yet the readers who find themselves in the post-Acts period may wonder whether the baptism of "Holy Spirit and of fire" of 3:16 is not to be understood, at the primary level of fulfillment in the story, as hendiadys (cf. Acts 2:2-4) and that John's expectations for the "mightier one" are wrong or at best misleading. Even more telling, immediately after the narrator closes his description of John's public preaching (3:18), he resorts to an almost bizarre use of prefiguration/foreshadowing in the plotted time to distance John's expectation from his own omniscient viewpoint: Herod "shuts up" John in prison *before* the description of all the *laos* being baptized (by John) and Jesus being baptized (by John) in solidarity with them (3:19-20). Again, not all is as it seems. In fact, might it not also be that it is John's imprisonment and eventual death (9:9) by Herod, the "king" of Israel, which forms the essence of John's preparing the "way" for "the anointed king" (3:4, 15; 2:11, 26; cf. 9:9; 23:8)? *(c)* Sandwiched in the story time between John's preaching and his arrest is a voice from heaven which accompanies the descent of the Holy Spirit upon Jesus (3:22a). Jesus is the "beloved Son," the one of Isa. 42:1, in whom God "takes pleasure" (3:22b). Thus both Gabriel's omniscient naming of Jesus as Son (1:32, 35) and the Isaianic-servant prophecies of Simeon and Anna are fused into one omniscient utterance (cf. "I have put my Spirit upon him," Isa. 42:1c—"the child to be born will be called holy, Son of God," Luke 1:35d).

3. The temptations (Luke 4:1-13) of Jesus are unequivocal in rejecting a way for the anointed Son as outlined in Mary's and Zechariah's expectations or hopes. Here Jesus' own point of view as a grown man (3:23) is given for the *first* time, as is the vantage of the quasi-divine negative, of the "slanderer"/"devil"—both within the omniscient framework of the narrator (cf. 4:1, 13). Such suggestions of the devil, Jesus retorts, are in fact tantamount to "tempting the Lord your God" (4:12b). Consequently it is now revealed that critical to the activity of the "anointed" Son will be a confrontation and "victory" over the cosmic power of evil that clearly differentiates this mission from the Davidic political or military overthrow of enemies (4:5; 10:17-20; 22:3,53b!).

4. Still in the power of the Spirit (cf. Luke 4:1), Jesus begins his public ministry in Galilee (Luke 4:14-15), "being glorified by all" (4:15). Yet, in the first detailed account of this ministry, at Nazareth (4:16-30), our narrator follows another summary of the positive *marveling* response to Jesus' presence by a sharply negative reaction from Jesus' *point of view* (4:22→4:23-27). Their enthusiasm, Jesus warns, reveals at base a people who refuse to repent when God sends his messengers, the prophets, to Israel, and in fact a people who demand "assurances" or demonstrable "signs" of Yahweh's presence in these emissaries. Therefore God goes outside Israel to take his salvation to non-Israel while passing over his "own" people. But now Jesus has just asserted that he is the *anointed* prophet of Isaiah 61 (Luke 4:18a, "Spirit *upon* me," cf. 3:22), who brings God's eschatological salvation to fulfillment! Two observations are worth making: *(a)* As in the temptation scene, our narrator presents Jesus as speaking for God, sc., Jesus' linking of the Nazareth congregation's response to himself to a typical response in Israel's history is *God's* perspective. Indeed, God is not "taken off guard" but will react as he has done with Israel in the past. *(b)* Second, Jesus is now speaking consciously about his own role in

Israel's history *as the anointed* prophet who has heard the voice from heaven declare him, "my Son," even as he has been anointed with the Spirit (cf. Acts 10:38). Clearly, for Jesus as the anointed one, Israel's enemies are not his (or God's) enemies. Thus when our narrator concludes with the volcanic hostility to kill Jesus (4:28-30), it appears that the fulfillment of eschatological salvation for Israel consists squarely in Israel's "victory"/killing of their own Messiah, especially since this viewpoint coincides with the omniscient perspective(s) of Simeon and Anna.

5.   The ensuing Galilean phase continues the ironic fulfillment of Mary's and Zechariah's prophecies as the "poor," handicapped, women, and foreigners accept Jesus Messiah on his own terms (e.g., Luke 5:12-16, 17-26, 27-32; 7:1-10; 8:1-3, 40-56). Thus it becomes true that God has indeed "put down the mighty from their thrones and exalted those of low degree." "Blessed are *you* poor, for the kingdom of God is [already] yours" (6:20b).

6.   If the reader is still in any doubt about what the narrator is up to in presenting the public or open fulfillment of Israel's salvation, John's own *doubting* from prison removes any uncertainty (Luke 7:18-23). In the "blind receiving their sight," "lepers being cleansed," "the dead being raised up," etc. (7:22), Israel is "being delivered from the hand of our enemies" (1:71a, 74a; cf. 4:18-20) in a definitive eschatological sense. For the "captives *are* being released," once and for all, from sin; those who are "oppressed" by satanic evil from every structure of society are being decisively liberated so that Israel's *consolation* is indeed of Israel, by Israel, and for Israel. Those who "take offense" at this way of fulfillment are, says Jesus, "less than the least in the kingdom of God" (7:28b).

7.   After sending out the Twelve (Luke 9:1-6) and as an immediate sequel to Jesus' feeding of the five thousand in the wilderness (9:10-17), our narrator has Peter speak for the disciples in proclaiming Jesus to be "the anointed one of God" (9:20). Jesus warns them not to use this name with anyone, going on to declare that the Son of man must *suffer* and be *killed* by the Sanhedrin in Jerusalem (9:22). And when we notice the disciples' "comprehension" following this "confession," we gain a greater appreciation for the rationale behind this command to silence: they sleep on the mountain when Jesus, Moses, and Elijah appear in *glory* and speak

about the exodus (death-departure) that Jesus must complete in Jerusalem (9:28-36), fail miserably at exorcising a demon as part of a "faithless and perverse generation" (9:41) at the base of the mountain (9:37-43a), and argue which of them is "the greatest," while trying to prevent others from (successfully!) exorcising demons "in Jesus' name" (9:46-50). Clearly *the disciples do not understand* who or what Jesus as "the Christ" or as "the chosen Son" (9:35→3:22→1:35; cf. 4:34,41; 8:28) is all about. After Jesus emphatically repeats the Son of man's impending doom (9:44), our narrator from his omniscient vantage point hardly needs to add—in four different phrases—that the disciples were completely "dense" to this understanding of "the Christ" (9:45). But now, curiously, one new element is introduced. It appears, in the passive participle of the second phrase, that there is a *divine* concealing and thus intention (and point of view) in their lack of understanding (cf. 8:10). At least it is now transparent that for the disciples to use the term, "the Christ," would not only be to deceive themselves, but also to mislead the crowds of Israel even further.

8. In the days of the Jerusalem ministry before his arrest, Jesus challenges the understanding of the people's leaders, the scribes (Luke 20:19,39,45) with respect to "the anointed one" (20:41-44). It is interesting that our narrator presents Jesus as arguing from a "point of view" within a Scripture quotation. (Since the *my* of "my Lord" must refer to David, who is speaking or composing the psalm, David has another "Lord" in addition to Lord Yahweh, 20:42-44; cf. 7:27.) According to Jesus, with this "Lord," David is referring to "the anointed one" so that the naming of Messiah as David's *son* (cf. 18:38) is at best misleading, at worst, a misnomer. Thus Jesus directly confronts the leaders' understanding of the Messiah by indirectly pointing to himself as the Son—of the demons' confession (4:34, 41; 8:28) and the heavenly voice(s) (3:22; 9:35). However the Christ may be "related" to David, it is clear that this "anointed one" transcends the popular notions of "son of David" as even David himself had confessed! Hence it is only fitting that the leaders (22:67; 23:2,35) and the people (23:18-23) hold Jesus accountable to their misguided, "diabolical" view right at the "hour" when they, along with the disciples (22:31-34,35-38,54-62) and the king of the Gentiles (cf. 22:25), clasp hands with "the authority of darkness" (22:53) to put the "anointed" Son (22:67,70) to death.

9. All the emphasis at the end of the first volume is directed to Jesus' own omniscient, definitive clarification of himself as the anointed Son: "O foolish folk, and sluggish of heart to believe all that the prophets have spoken. Was it not a divine necessity that 'the anointed one' suffer these things in order to enter into his glory?" (24:25-26). And the narrator adds, "And beginning with Moses and all the prophets, he interpreted to them in all the Scriptures the things concerning himself" (24:27). A second time Jesus declares directly what is at the heart of his being "the Christ" (24:46). All the Scriptures point to the suffering of the Christ in God's plan for the consummation of Israel's salvation and for the light of salvation to the Gentiles (24:47; "my Father," 24:49; cf. Acts 2:23). Thus at the center of all the scriptural voices are the suffering-servant passages of Isaiah (see especially Luke 22:37, quoting Isa. 53:12 as the *goal* of Jesus' entire ministry) and not the images of the victorious rule of David and his powerful "horn of salvation" (1:69). The omniscience of our narrator has combined with the omniscience of the central character of the plot, who, according to his own divinely inspired speech (10:21), declares that he as "Son" alone has the knowledge to reveal the "mind" of God (10:22).[24]

THE GENTILES AND ISRAEL'S DESTINY

Thus it cannot be that the fundamental resolution has yet to be made. Tiede's pattern of hope/promise(s) (Luke 1–2)→confrontation/"falling" of willful Israel, with only some/inaugurated "rising" (Luke 3—Acts 28)→primary/fundamental fulfillment (beyond Acts 28) simply is *not* true to the preponderate emphasis of Luke-Acts that salvation is realized for Israel precisely through Israel's rejection of Messiah. But what of Israel's rejection in the Acts that seems to have taken on monolithic proportions by the end of the story? Is Luke the historian de facto forced to "write off" eschatological salvation for the overwhelming majority of Israel, despite his fundamental resolution?

1. *The Servant Pattern*

Both Tiede and Tannehill[25] are correct in pointing to the servant passages of Isaiah as literarily and theologically constitutive for much of the story material of Acts. But again Luke's primary perspective in his use of this pattern is lost in both proposals. As in the second (Isa. 49:1-6), (third) and fourth (52:13—53:12) servant songs, so it is clear also in Luke's portrayal that Israel/Jacob/"tribes of Israel" are being restored by the servant's mission of bringing eschatological salvation to an Israel that for the most part violently rejects this mission.

a. Restored Israel. As in Isa. 49:1-6 (especially 49:3-4), where the servant as both an individual and a corporate remnant, "Israel" (49:4), takes the eschatological mission/message to the rest of rejecting Israel, so also in Acts the narrator takes pains to describe the Israel that responds even to the end of Acts 28 as the restored, fulfilled people of final salvation that carries on the servant mission to a hard-hearted remainder of the nation. It is simply not true that Acts 21:20 and the "myriads[26] of Jews who are believers" refers back exclusively to the period of Acts 1–5 so that Luke traces an epochal or historical development of rejection. Even a cursory reading of Acts shows that the summaries of 9:31 and 12:24 describe a continuing growth of the ranks in the Judean and Jerusalem churches as well as in Samaria and, interestingly (9:31), in Galilee. Acts 12:24 in particular closes the events of Acts 12 that depict the Jerusalem church and summarizes developments in Judea and in the Cornelius and Antioch missions. The use of *auxanō* and *plēthynomai* in Acts 12:24 with the *logos tou theou* links this swelling of the numbers to the related cluster of ideas and vocabulary of other summaries of church growth, as in 6:7; cf. 9:31; 19:20; (7:17). Moreover, 9:31 excludes the impression that it is Gentiles instead of Jews who are being added as messianic believers, since in Luke's schema the Gentile mission has yet to begin. And when the summary of 16:5 is added—following Paul's return to Lystra and other cities where there are both Jewish and Gentile believers—and our narrator states that "the churches increased *(perisseuō)* in numbers daily," then the theory of "no second chance" for repentance, as propounded by Jack T. Sanders, becomes untenable.[27] Consequently, Luke is stressing that the eschatological believing Israel is not inconsiderable and in absolute numbers is quite large; the "tent/booth of David" has indeed been "restored" *(anorthoō,* 15:16-17).

b. Glory of Israel. The second servant song (Isa. 49:1-6) announces the preposterous idea that Yahweh "will be glorified" in the servant's (both individual and corporate) rejection and humiliation by Israel as a whole (49:3-4, 6). A number of passages throughout Deutero-Isaiah link this glory, which only God and no other has, to Israel's eschatological salvation, which is displayed in the presence of and offered to the nations of the earth (Isa. 40:5—cf. Luke 3:4-6; Isa. 42:12; 43:7, cf. 43:9; 45:25; 46:13; cf. 48:11). But it is a glory not only that Israel does *not* recognize but also which Israel violently tries to remove as an abomination to God, as the third and especially the fourth songs divulge (52:14; 53:2). Nevertheless, it is exactly through the hostility against and suffering of a part of Israel, the servant, that Israel as a whole is and will be gathered and the very means by which the Gentiles are incorporated into Israel's eschatological salvation.

This is the pattern operative in Acts, as the Lukan Paul makes clear in such passages as the following:

- Acts 14:22—"only through tribulations we must *(dei)* enter the kingdom of God."
- Acts 13:47—through Antiochian Jews' rejection/hostility Paul and cohorts are the corporate servant through which the individual servant, i.e., "Lord," brings salvation to the ends of the earth (Isa. 49:6).
- Acts 13:48—the Gentile believers give glory to God, just as Isa. 42:12 and other passages prophesy!
- Acts 26:21-23—Paul summarizes his calling as that of the servant mission whereby the suffering of Messiah continues, even as he, Messiah, as the first of the resurrected, continues to bring salvation both to Israel and the nations through the violent rejection of Paul which culminates in the temple seizure.

Israel's glory consists not simply or even primarily in bringing revelation to the Gentiles, as apparently Tiede perceives it, but rather, more fundamentally in the very mission of dividing Israel through hostility and suffering. Thus again the central message of Acts *with respect to Israel* is that God's *boulē* (2:23) of salvation has been and is being fulfilled of, by, and for Israel. Again the tension between promise and fulfillment is fundamentally ironic: Israel's rejection actually engenders Israel's glory. Therefore, though from a human perspective the anguish, division, even killing experienced within Israel is "tragic," yet from the divine intention (e.g., prophecy/

Scripture) "tragedy" is at best a misnomer to describe the story of Israel in Luke-Acts.

2. The Deuteronomistic Pattern

But what, finally, of the even greater and growing myriads of Israel that are rejecting their salvation as it extends to the end of the earth? And what of the expectation of Mary and Zechariah (and the disappointed disciples, Luke 24:21)? Is there not finally in Luke's schema a literal fulfillment of these? Is Acts 1:6 after all hardly an "idle" question?[28]

I have argued elsewhere that Luke comprehends Israel's story in Luke-Acts within the Deuteronomistic view of Israel's history of the rejection of the prophets sent to them as God's mediators of redemption/salvation.[29] Jesus, together with the apostles/witnesses in Acts who share his fate of rejection or even death, represents the crowning point of this sending. That is to say, the unrelenting history of stubborn resistance is broken decisively, eschatologically, in the death of the prophet like Moses and, through his being raised up from the dead, Israel a second time is offered the opportunity of repentance. Hence the familiar pattern, persistent disobedience—destruction and exile—repentance—return/vindication, attested in many Jewish intertestamental Palestinian texts, is radically altered even as it is proleptically terminated. Most illuminating in this respect is the way that Luke alone presents the disciples after Jesus' exaltation—through Jesus' own apocalyptic prospect (Luke 21)—as escaping the final destruction of Jerusalem, which will fulfill God's wrath upon a disobedient people (Luke 21:8-36). The church, therefore, as the final restored remnant of Israel, becomes the beacon of hope as light both to Gentiles and to unrepentant Israel. Paul's use of Isaiah 6 in Acts 28 is a classic formulation of the Deuteronomistic pattern. Although its solemn finality surely decrees an inevitable disaster upon a monolith of rejection that has formed again, parallel to the gospel, yet it also spells hope if Israel repents. Luke 21 again is crucial if, as is indicated especially in the imagery and vocabulary of 21:21-24, Luke has Deuteronomy 31 and 32 (the Song of Moses) in mind—a capsule of the Deuteronomistic historians' retrospect and prospect. Here Gentile destruction and exile of Israel "in the final days" (*ep' eschatōn [hēmerōn]*, 32:20) is followed by a universal judgment and restoration/vindication of all

Israel.[30] Thus again the servant pattern is illuminative. Isaiah 49:1-6 displays the main outlines of the Deuteronomistic pattern but now stresses that the servant as a restored remnant will indeed be successful in bringing the twelve tribes back to Yahweh. The LXX even more than the MT accents this ultimate return of Israel when in the first person the corporate servant speaks, "I shall be gathered and glorified (vindicated) before the Lord" (Isa. 49:5b) in the mission of gathering all Israel to Yahweh. Far from sounding certain and ultimate doom for Israel as a whole, Paul in Acts 28:26-28 declares unflinchingly that the promises of God surely shall prevail.

4

THE JEWISH PEOPLE
IN LUKE-ACTS

Jack T. Sanders

What, exactly, does Luke think of the Jewish people as a whole, of "the Jews"? When we ask this question we do not receive back an easy answer; for sometimes it seems that only the religious leaders are guilty of having executed Jesus, and sometimes it seems that all the inhabitants of Jerusalem—or even all Jews everywhere—share in the guilt; and the accusations of hostility to the purposes of God seem sometimes to be directed specifically at the religious authorities and at other times to be thrown around indiscriminately at all Jews in sight. Thus it is clear that temple authorities arrested Jesus and brought about his death, but Paul says, in Acts 13:27, that "those dwelling in Jerusalem *and* their rulers" did it; and the conclusion of Stephen's speech seems to involve all Jews, since it accuses, without qualification, all descendants of the ancient Israelites: "Whom of the prophets did your fathers not persecute? And they killed those who proclaimed beforehand the coming of the Righteous One, whose deliverers and murderers now you have become" (Acts 7:52). When Stephen then (7:53) refers to these deliverers and murderers as those who had "received the Law," this seems even more to indicate all Jews, or at least all religious ones, than to refer only to the chief priests.

This same passage may be cited again as an example of the way in which Luke sometimes seems to indicate all the Jewish people as those hostile to the divine purpose; and we may also note in this connection the repeated and, after a time, predictable—although not universal—hostility to Paul's preaching in the Diaspora synagogues.

Otherwise, however, Luke 19:48 explains that the fact that "the entire people *(ho laos hapas)"* was "hanging on [Jesus'] every word" was what at first prevented the temple authorities from arresting Jesus; and Acts 2:47 claims that the apostles were "standing in good stead with the whole people *(holos ho laos)."*

And what are we to make of the fact that in Antioch, in Corinth, and in Rome, Paul "persuades" *(peithei)* (13:43; 18:4; 28:23) Jews in his audience but then each time condemns them in quite general terms and announces that the gospel is to be taken to the Gentiles? If one explains that, of course, Jewish opposition to Paul developed after his successful "persuasion" in Antioch and Corinth, prompting Paul's condemnation, then the inquirer will be forced to respond in turn that the pattern of persuasion followed by condemnation and rejection is repeated in the final scene in Acts *without* the benefit of that hostility.

These inconsistencies show that the Lukan portrait of "the Jews" is not done in vividly contrasting colors but in subtle shades. What *does* Luke think of the Jewish people? Of course, we are not thinking of such items as whether they are rich or poor, or what their table manners were. We are thinking of such issues as these: Does Luke see the Jewish people as guilty in the death of Jesus or not, as irredeemably opposed to the will of God or not, as recipients of the salvation of God or not? Inasmuch as these issues have received no small discussion in modern scholarly writing, we may perhaps be helped on our way by a brief examination of the alternatives posed by other scholars regarding this topic.

While several different opinions are current, there are nevertheless, in the main and broadly speaking, only two choices. (For the sake of space, we must omit here discussion of variations within the two options.) Either Luke intends to distinguish between those Jews who accept the gospel and become Christians and those who do not, in which case he hardly separates the latter group from their religious leaders and condemns them together, or he does not make this distinction and condemns all the Jewish people collectively for their obstinacy in the face of the divine proffering of salvation and for their participation in the execution of Jesus. The former view is today—in this country, in any case—often connected with the name of Jacob Jervell, and the latter is probably most normally associated with the name of Ernst Haenchen, although it is widely enough held that Jervell has referred to it as a "common opinion."[1] We proceed to a brief consideration of these two possibilities and then to a further analysis of the Lukan portrayal of "the Jews," in the course of which analysis we shall, so we hope, be able to open up some new possibilities of interpretation. First, the "common opinion."

The view that Luke condemns "the Jews"—that is, the Jewish people considered together as a group, without any distinctions among them—and "writes them off" is almost as old as critical New Testament scholarship.[2] Franz Overbeck, in rejecting the explanation of Acts given by the Tübingen school (that the purpose of Acts was to reconcile apostolic Jewish Christianity and Pauline Gentile Christianity),[3] took such a view,[4] as did Alfred Loisy a few years later.[5] In more recent times, Ernst Haenchen has continued this interpretation of the role of the Jews in Acts. According to him, the opposition between Judaism and Christianity, which centers on the issue of the Christian proclamation of the resurrection,[6] develops as Acts progresses. At first (Acts 3–5), the church expands and enjoys the good will of the people while experiencing the opposition only of the religious leaders.[7] With Stephen, however, the situation changes. Stephen's speech is "filled" with unmistakable "aggressiveness and palpitating wrath against the Jewish people," the purpose of which is to distinguish Christianity, as the group in continuity with the Old Testament, from the Jews, whose rejection of Jesus and the gospel shows them to be an "aberration."[8] Acts 8–11 then shifts the story line from the Jewish mission to the Gentile mission,[9] at the beginning of which the attitude toward the Jewish *people* is completely reversed from that in Acts 3–5, for in 12:3 "the Jews" favor persecution of the Christians. "Here, therefore, the people are no longer on the side of the Christians, as formerly—according to the Lukan presentation."[10] From this point on, "the Jews" oppose Christianity. Paul's first missionary sermon concludes with a rejection of the Jewish mission (Acts 13:46), a rejection which, while it refers in the first case only to the Antiochene Jews, has general significance.[11] After this, "the entire course of the life of the Christian missionary Paul is determined by the arguments with the Jews,"[12] the standard synagogue scenes of Paul's ministry being done in "placard style." It is the purpose of the apostolic council in Acts to be the "watershed" of this movement from the Jews to the Gentiles.[13] Paul's arrest in Jerusalem provides the opportunity to show him in conflict with Palestinian Judaism as well,[14] and the final scene, with Paul in Rome, represents for Luke "a final rejection of Israel and its being replaced with the Gentiles."[15] Thus Luke expresses "the theology of Gentile Christianity toward the end of the first century . . .; [this theology] no longer sees any sense or any truth in Israel's election." "Luke has written the Jews off."[16]

Briefly summarized, then, Haenchen's explanation is that, while Luke recognized that the first Christians were Jews and that there was a (successful) Jewish mission in the first days of Christianity, the purpose of Acts is to show how things developed from that stage to the situation in which Luke lived, i.e., a situation in which Christians were Gentiles and in which Jews opposed Christianity. Or, to use Haenchen's words, "In reality Luke the historian is wrestling [in Acts], from the first page to the last, with the problem of the *mission to the Gentiles without the Law.*"[17] While Haenchen did not give much attention to the Gospel of Luke in his explanations of Acts, it would not be inconsistent with his position to see the Gospel as also displaying the same tendencies as the Acts, inasmuch as the Gospel also begins with a pronounced friendliness toward Jewish religion and then moves from that harmony to conflict and rejection (the passion narrative, of course, but also Jesus' rejection in his hometown, Luke 4:16-30), with tips along the way about the Gentile mission climaxing with Luke 24:47, ". . . to all the Gentiles." Haenchen's explanation of the Lukan portrayal of the Jews would therefore allow one to see that there is an order to the way in which Luke has portrayed the Jewish people. It is not that they appear indiscriminately sometimes as friendly and sometimes as hostile, now the recipients of salvation and now rejected; rather, they fit into these various molds *according to Luke's plan of historical development.*

The other way of explaining the Lukan portrayal of the Jewish people, that Luke does distinguish among the Jews as a group and that he intends to condemn only those who do not accept the gospel, while it may not be the "common opinion," is nevertheless the explanation given by some of the better known and esteemed New Testament scholars, and may in fact be the view of the majority. This view goes back to Adolf Harnack[18] and has been proposed, in one form or another, by Hans Conzelmann, Augustin George, and

Jacob Jervell.[19] Probably the most persuasive advocate of this position, however, is Gerhard Lohfink. Beginning from the observation that the prophecy of Simeon in Luke 2:34 ("He is set for the fall and rise of many in Israel") presents the Lukan thesis of the *krisis* of Israel, Lohfink proceeds to show how people respond to this *krisis* and how, consequently, the "true Israel" is determined.[20] Thus the "identity of Israel-church" is carried out in Acts, after Jesus has first, in the Gospel, addressed "all Israel,"[21] which address to Israel comes to a head in Jesus' addressing Jerusalem in the passion narrative, where "all Israel is . . . gathered."[22] Whereas, in general, the split produced in Israel by Jesus' address is a split between people and leaders, still the people unite with the leaders in Pilate's court, so 'that the grounds for repentance, so necessary in Acts, can be laid.[23]

While the speeches in Acts, as well as those of Jesus in the Gospel, especially Jesus' sermon in Nazareth, present a blanket denunciation of the Jews for the killing of Jesus and therefore do not coincide with the division here described, the reason for the discrepancy is, according to Lohfink, that Luke is merely quoting sources in the speeches.[24] The apostles in the first part of Acts, however, again "address . . . all Israel" in the temple, just as Jesus had done in Jerusalem at the end of the Gospel, and the enormous numbers of conversions in Acts show that the "gathering of Israel," begun by Jesus, is now carried out.[25] This "positive presentation ends at 5:42," however, and the martyrdom of Stephen marks the change from positive to negative Jewish response.[26] Thus Lohfink explains, "In the period of the first apostolic preaching, the true Israel was gathered out of the Jewish people! And that Israel that remained rigid in its rejection of Jesus lost its right to be the true people of God; it became Judaism."[27] From this point and forward in Acts, the gospel message goes to the Gentiles, since "the true Israel is attained only when the Gentiles have been brought into the community of the people of God."[28]

These two explanations of the portrayal of the Jews in Luke-Acts are so different that one almost wonders if the representatives of the two opposing views have been reading the same edition! Obviously, if we now want to try to make our way through this thicket of different opinions to a clearer understanding of Luke's attitude toward "the Jews," toward the Jewish people as a collective entity—

or, to put the issue in perhaps a more neutral way, to a satisfactory understanding of Luke's portrayal of the Jewish people, *including* whether he thinks of them as a collective entity—we shall have to pick our way by taking careful notice of the often confusing path-markers—that is, of what the Jewish people say and do in Luke-Acts and of what is said about them. At the same time, we shall also want to keep in mind that a successful negotiation of the thicket will likely bring us out upon one of two clearings, that which allows us to see that Luke thought that all Jews were perverse, or that which provides a perspective showing that he intended to represent only those who rejected Christianity as perverse. We begin with the most obvious signposts.

One point on which there need be no confusion is whether Luke makes distinctions of any kind among the Jews. Naturally he does. We may merely refer to his characterization of the various Jewish religious leaders in the latter part of the Gospel; also, toward the end of Acts he makes much out of the differences between the Pharisees, who believed in a resurrection from the dead, and Sadducees, who did not. Furthermore, as Lohfink has pointed out, Luke underscores the fact that many Jews converted to Christianity in its early days in Jerusalem, whereas others did not. That Luke wants to emphasize that point is seen in the last of the summary statements in Acts about conversions (21:20), where he has James refer to the "many myriads of believers . . . among the Jews." Furthermore, throughout the course of Paul's mission, Luke consistently refers to both Jewish and Gentile response to Paul's preaching, and he some-times notes that some of the Jews "believed" (Acts 14:1; 17:11-12; 18:8). Thus, that some Jews became Christians while others did not is one point in Acts that no one could overlook.

In the second place, it is also abundantly clear that Luke uses the term "people of God," or just "people," to mean the church,[29] and that he thinks that the direct line runs from Moses and the prophets through John the Baptist and Jesus to Christianity, and not in some other direction.[30] It is again on the lips of James that we see this most plainly. In Acts 15:14, as a way of resolving the disagreement in the apostolic council, James states that "Simeon has explained how at first God oversaw taking out of the Gentiles *a people* for his name"; and that Luke knows that he is using a quasi-technical term is seen in his considered use of the term "people of Israel" (Luke

2:32; Acts 4:10; 13:17, 24; and especially 4:27, "Gentiles and peoples of Israel"). Most significant, however, is the repeated use of the absolute *ho laos* by Paul in Acts 26:17,23. When Paul says here that the Lord confirmed to him that he was "saving [or 'choosing'] [Paul] from *the people* and from the Gentiles," and when he then affirms that it was according to prophecy that Christ should "proclaim light to *the people* and to the Gentiles," "the people" obviously means "the people of Israel." But, when the Lord says to Paul in a dream in Acts 18:10, "I have a numerous people in this city," he means the church, made up, as 18:7-8 had explained, of Jews *and* Gentiles. Thus Luke understands that he is shifting the pre-Christian understanding of people of God as people of Israel to the Christian understanding of people of God as Christians.[31] "The Law grew smoothly and naturally into the gospel."[32]

Along with this goes Luke's fairly unconvincing apologetic that the Christian belief in the resurrection (of Jesus) is in reality the familiar Pharisaic belief in the (coming) resurrection. Paul makes this point in Acts 26:6, and it is the rationale for his acquittal in the Sanhedrin (Acts 23:6-10). Whether it is correct to maintain in this connection that Luke thinks of the church as "Israel" is not so certain. Luke never uses such a term, and "people of Israel" (Acts 13:24) or just "Israel" (Acts 1:6) always means "the Jews." Perhaps, as long as we remind ourselves that what Lohfink means by "Israel" is what Luke meant by "people of God," i.e., the people through whom and to whom God's salvation has come, we may proceed without objecting to such an explanation of the theology of Luke-Acts. The explanation given by Joseph A. Fitzmyer seems to fit the evidence better.[33] According to him, the author of Acts emphasizes that the first Christians were Jews but that they were "marked off from the Jewish people as such"; and he maintains only that Acts "vaguely suggests" that the church was the new Israel.

The logical conclusion to be drawn from these two fairly obvious points—that Luke knows one Jew from another and that he thinks of the church and not of the contemporary non-Christian Jews as being in direct continuity with the former holy people of God—is that Luke does, indeed, have a "divided Israel" theory, according to which the non-Christian Jews, not the Christians, are the aberration. The condemnation announced by Paul and Barnabas in Antioch, "It was necessary for the word of God to be spoken to you first. Since you reject it and judge yourselves not worthy of eternal life, behold, we turn to the Gentiles" (Acts 13:46), would seem to fit this conclusion well. Alas, however, we cannot finish with the matter so easily; for, in addition to the evidence that exists in support of the "divided Israel" theory, there exists in Luke-Acts a considerable body of evidence of the "blanket condemnation" variety, according to which Jews are by nature and congenitally obstreperous and opposed to the will and purposes of God and have been, as a group and as a nation, excluded from God's salvation. Stephen's speech and Paul's last condemnation of the Jews at the end of Acts are ready examples. But this has been the problem all along! The reason that there are two theories about Luke on the Jews is that Luke-Acts presents both kinds of evidence, sometimes back-to-back. Why?

We may dispense briefly with the explanation that Luke's use of different sources accounts for his differing presentations of the Jews.[34] The older redaction theory of Loisy, according to which the anti-Judaic statements in Luke-Acts are the result of redactional activity, was an attempt to deal in those terms with what seems to be Luke's divided attitude toward the Jews.[35] But this putative "redactor" would be, after all, the person responsible for the final form of Luke-Acts, the work that we are considering here, so that the question must then be addressed to him. Why does the person responsible for the final form of Luke-Acts seem to hold both the view that the Jews are uniformly bad and a theory of a "divided Israel" at the same time? To pose the question specifically in terms of Lohfink's analysis, outlined above: Why does Luke create a narrative that tells the story of the gathering of Israel and then include speeches from first to last that seem to support the other view, even if he did get the speeches from some separate source? Source and redaction theories, unfortunately, do not answer our question; they only deal with the process of becoming.

Lohfink has, in fact, provided the key to the solution of this riddle: to separate speech from narrative in Luke-Acts. When we consider what Luke has his main characters (Jesus, Peter, Stephen,[36] and Paul) say about "the Jews," apart from any consideration of the story line, and when we then look at how "the Jews" behave in the narrative without reference to what the main characters say about them, all the evidence will fall into place.

Let us consider first the speeches in Acts. Stephen's closing tirade, which gets him lynched, encapsulates the position.

> Hard-necked and uncircumcised in hearts and ears, you always thrust against the Holy Spirit; as your fathers, so you. Whom of the prophets did your fathers not persecute? And they killed those who proclaimed beforehand the coming of the Righteous One, whose deliverers and murderers now you have become, you who received the Law in angelic ordinances; and you did not keep it.[37]

These accusations seem to be directed to the Jewish people generally, not merely to the members of the Sanhedrin, who are described as trying him. The descendants of the Jewish ancestors "always" oppose the divine will, although they are the recipients of the Law.[38] That charge can hardly be limited to the religious leaders,[39] even if the charge of persecuting the prophets may be read to admit the possibility that some Israelites, in any case—namely, the prophets themselves—were not subject to this bent.[40]

It is not only in Stephen's speech, however, that such accusations occur. Peter, in Acts 2:36, says to "all the house of Israel," "You crucified" Jesus; and Peter likewise accuses "all the people of Israel" in Acts 4:10, charging, "You crucified" him. In the next breath he inserts the word "you" into a psalm proof-text so that it is quoted to say, "The stone that was considered of no account by *you* the builders . . ." (4:11). Thus the charge of crucifixion in Acts 5:30, which is, according to the verisimilitude of the scene, directed at the Sanhedrin, could just as well be intended for "all the house" or for "all the people of Israel." Even in the speech to Cornelius, Acts 10:39, Peter cannot omit this charge and says that "they did away with him" by crucifixion. Since Peter had just referred to "all that [Jesus] did in the region of the Jews and Jerusalem," there can be little doubt who "they" are.[41] Especially in this speech to the first truly Gentile convert in Acts, we see how Luke builds up the image of general Jewish guilt in the death of Jesus simply by omitting subjects for the verbs. It would have been easy enough to write that the Sanhedrin or the chief priests did away with Jesus, but Luke does not do that; so, since he had just written that Jesus worked among the Jews, what is the Gentile reader to think but that "the Jews" killed Jesus?

But does Luke not alleviate this charge of having killed Jesus, made repeatedly in the speeches in Acts, with an excuse? Does he not twice (3:17; 13:27) say that the Jews acted only out of ignorance? And does he not thereby imply that if the hearers repent and believe they may escape their just deserts? These two passages require a little closer scrutiny. Peter's speech in Acts 3, addressed to "all the people" (3:11), indeed allows that they "and [their] rulers . . . acted in ignorance" (3:17) when they "killed the Prince of Life" (3:15). (We cannot avoid noting that here Peter thus indicts *both* people *and* rulers as those who killed Jesus.) Peter then immediately (3:19) challenges them to "repent and turn about." The second occurrence of the ignorance theme, however—in Paul's first speech—is hardly the same, for the ignorance appears here in the third rather than in the second person. Whereas Peter had challenged the entire Jewish people with their guilt and had in that connection offered them the opportunity to repent and convert, Paul refers his Antiochene hearers back to the Jews in Jerusalem ("those dwelling in Jerusalem and their rulers," 13:27), who are said not to have *acted* in ignorance (as in 3:17), but to have been ignorant of "him,"[42] *although they "read the voices of the prophets every Sabbath"* (13:27). These they then "fulfilled by condemning" Jesus; yet it is impossible for the reader to misunderstand who is really condemned here. It is those Jerusalem Jews who did not have the sense to understand their own Scriptures.[43] After this, Paul moves fairly rapidly toward a pitch for the Antiochene Jews to convert (13:32-41). Surely we are seeing here, therefore, Luke's epochal scheme at work. When the Jerusalem Jews are confronted with their sin and ignorance, they are given the opportunity to convert. After the Gentile mission begins, Jerusalemite ignorance provides no further opportunity for Jerusalemite conversion but is rather a judgment upon Jerusalem and its inhabitants. This reference back, however, to the condemnation of Jerusalemite Jews for their now inexcusable ignorance provides the incentive for the conversion of Antiochene Jews. I believe that it would be correct to say that, in Luke's opinion, after Paul's sermon in Acts 13, the Antiochene Jews also have no excuse.[44] In a word, the proclamation of the gospel both offers the opportunity for repentance and removes the excuse of ignorance. Thus, if we continue to ignore the story line and concentrate on what Paul says, we see that he is very shortly pronouncing God's rejection also upon the

Antiochene Jews in the first of the three announcements of the turning to the Gentiles: "To you it was necessary first to speak the word of God. Since you reject it and judge yourselves not worthy of eternal life, behold, we turn to the Gentiles" (13:46).[45]

After that, Paul does not speak to or about "the Jews" again until he is in Corinth delivering the second such announcement: "Your blood be upon your head! I am clean. From now on I will go to the Gentiles" (18:6). Why their own blood? Surely because, by having rejected the gospel, they have sealed their own fate. But "the Jews" (18:5) of Corinth had not participated in the death of Jesus; they had only "opposed" and "blasphemed" (18:6)! No matter; when Jews in Paul's Diaspora mission reject the gospel they fall under the same condemnation that is pronounced against those in Jerusalem (13:27) who actually carried out the deed. Furthermore, when the Lukan Paul mentions in 20:19, in what is almost an offhand manner, the various Jewish "counsels" (or "plots") that have brought him "tears and trials," he is declaring that "the Jews" have regularly hindered his mission. After Paul is arrested, while he once explains that it was "the high priest . . . and all the presbyterium" that gave him his earlier authority to persecute Christians (22:5), still, when the time comes for him to speak before Agrippa, he says simply that he was "accused by Jews" (26:2); and he adds that it was "Jews" who "tried to slay [him] in the temple" (26:21).

Finally, in Paul's last speech, the conclusion and denouement of Acts, after Paul has again accused "the Jews" (28:19) for his imprisonment, the Roman Jews are condemned with a scriptural quotation for their intransigent and endemic ignorance,[46] and Paul gives up on them.[47] That this condemnation applies probably to all Jews and not just to Paul's Roman hearers is seen in the existence of the condemnation within Scripture (Isaiah), in the address of the scriptural passage to "this people" (Acts 28:26), and, of course, in the position of the condemnation at the conclusion of Luke-Acts. "Luke has written the Jews off."[48] Thus the witness of the speeches in Acts is that the Jews generally are irredeemably resistant to God's will and his offer of salvation, and that they are the murderers of Jesus. When these charges are reduced, in the case of the allowance of the extenuating circumstance of ignorance in Acts 3:27, the purpose is to provide the opportunity for conversion to Christianity; but there seem to be no second chances, once such opportunities are past.

Having examined what the speeches in Acts say about the Jews, we now need to give some attention to the *role* or *function* of the missionary speeches (all of Peter's sermons and Paul's sermons at Antioch and Athens) within Luke-Acts, although this discussion will take us briefly away from our analysis of what the leading characters in Luke-Acts *say* about Jews. According to Ulrich Wilckens, the purpose of all these speeches is to provoke repentance among the Jewish listeners. In this way, Luke sets up an *"ordo salutis"* as "a comprehensive and normative view of repentance generally,"[49] i.e., for everyone. Unfortunately, Wilckens has failed to deal with three aspects of the issue. One is that Stephen's speech includes no call to repentance,[50] whereas the missionary sermons do (presumably it is implied in Stephen's speech). Another, however, is that the accusation against the Jews is maintained even when there are only Gentiles in the audience (Acts 10:39), a fact that ruins the connection between guilt and repentance and, consequently, the *ordo salutis* pattern.[51] The third problem overlooked by Wilckens is the response of Jews to these missionary sermons, which is the main issue with which we need to deal at this point. While it is true that many Jews respond favorably to these missionary sermons prior to the Stephen episode, from that point on they generally do not, and Paul's first missionary sermon, in fact, also becomes the occasion of the first of his three statements of condemnation of the Jews and of turning to the Gentiles (Acts 13:46). Thus the *function* of the missionary speeches in Acts *as regards the Jews* is not to set up an *ordo salutis* (although such a pattern in general terms, that is, regarding the Gentiles, is probably—indeed, very likely—part of Luke's purpose); it is rather to show that, after the initial positive response in the first five chapters of Acts, the Jews *reject* the gospel.[52] Since the Stephen episode marks the demise of the "Jerusalem springtime" (Lohfink), Stephen's speech neither includes nor implies any call to repentance.[53]

What, then, do the sayings of Jesus in the Gospel have to do with "the Jews"? When the public ministry opens, we find Jesus prophesying in the synagogue at Nazareth that his audience will one day mock him with the call, "Physician, heal yourself" (Luke 4:23). This prophecy is more or less fulfilled in Jerusalem (Luke 23:35) when the *rulers* say, "He saved others, let him save himself." But the connection between Jesus' audience in Nazareth, to whom the prophecy is made, and those in Jerusalem who fulfill the prophecy is that they are Jews, not that they are Nazarenes or rulers. The prophecy that Jesus gives in Nazareth, therefore, must be pointed at Jews in general, not just at Nazarenes or at Jewish rulers. In this same speech, then, Jesus goes on to refer pointedly to two of Israel's better-known prophets, Elijah and Elisha, who helped *non-Israelites* in need but not Israelites in similar straits. Since Elijah and Elisha are referred to here in their roles of prophet as physician, the implication is overwhelming that the prophet Jesus, who has just referred to himself as a physician, is also sent to Gentiles and not to Jews. Thus the two-sided Jewish rejection, the Jews' rejection of and by God, is established in this, Jesus' opening address in the Gospel, "perhaps the most significant passage in Luke-Acts."[54] Further statements of Jesus in the same vein, to list them briefly, are to be found in Luke 7:9, where Jesus heals a centurion's slave and declares that he "has not even found such faith in Israel";[55] in 10:13-15, where Jesus closes the books on the locales of his now-finished Galilean ministry, which are now doomed because they did not repent; and probably in 7:31-34; 11:29-32; 17:25, where "this generation" that is condemned is apparently "this *Jewish* generation."[56]

Further, the saying about "this generation" that is worked into the woe upon the "legists" (Luke 11:47-51) obviously has a general application and is not understood as applying only to the legists. Here, Jesus observes that "you build the tombs of the prophets, but your fathers killed them"; thus "you consent to the deeds of your fathers, since they killed them and you build" (11:47-48). Furthermore, "The Wisdom of God said, 'I will send them prophets and apostles, and they will kill and persecute some of them, so that *the blood of all the prophets* shed from the foundation of the world *may be required of this generation*'" (11:49-50). Jesus then underscores this saying by adding, "Truly I say to you, it will be required of this generation" (11:51). Thus the condemnations of Stephen's speech and of Paul's telling the Corinthian Jews that their "blood will be upon [their] head" represent no new perspective in the Acts. They are entirely in harmony with the pronouncements of Jesus himself. Finally, those who think that they are in the kingdom of God but in reality are excluded (Luke 13:23-30) can only be "the Jews," since the excluded point out in their defense that Jesus "taught in [their] streets" (13:26), and since others will come from all directions (13:29) to enter the kingdom left vacant by the excluded.[57]

As the Gospel approaches its climax, the Lukan Jesus begins increasingly to use parables to express the condemnation of the Jewish people. In fact, Luke uses several parables that appear in the travel narrative—probably all the better-known ones[58]—as further occasions for Jesus to condemn and pronounce judgment upon the Jews.[59] Naturally, this use of these parables has nothing to do with their blessed original meaning.

The first of these is the parable of the banquet (Luke 14:16-24). While we must forgo here a full consideration of this parable, we are able to see that, however the argument between those who find three groups allegorized in the Lukan form of the parable and those who find two may finally be concluded,[60] the first group, the originally invited, surely represents the Jews and their rejection of and then by God. The invited give their silly excuses, they reject the invitation, and thus they receive the judgment, "None of those invited men will taste my supper" (14:24).[61] The parable of the rich man and Lazarus, further, provides the Lukan Jesus the opportunity to make a point similar to that which the Lukan Paul later makes in Acts 13:27; for there is no other help possible for the surviving relatives of the rich man in hell, who are doomed to follow him there if they do not change, inasmuch as they already "have Moses and the prophets" (Luke 16:29). As Paul later says, they cannot understand these Scriptures even though they read them regularly. Thus, "If they do not hear Moses and the prophets, they will not be persuaded even if one rise from the dead" (16:31). Since Luke, of course, knows who rose from the dead, this conclusion to the parable is about as clear a statement as he could give of the Christian opinion that the Jews are intrinsically stubborn, intransigent, and closed-minded.[62] Similarly, the uniquely Lukan portions of the parable of the pounds (Luke 19:11-27) seem to be directed against "the Jews."[63] Here the nobleman is Jesus, his kingdom is the kingdom of God, those who send an embassy seeking to thwart his accession to dominion over them (19:14) are the Jews, and the execution of these rebels upon the return of the nobleman-now-become-king (19:27) is the well-merited destruction of the Jews at the second coming. While the position of this parable within the Gospel might lead one to think of it as referring only to the destruction of Jerusalem, not to the destruction of the Jewish people, the problem of such an interpretation is that the destruction seems to be deferred to the second coming.[64] The parable seems not to leave the time of its conclusion in doubt, since the new king has returned from his journey, having received his kingdom, and has meted out justice to his earthly representatives (19:15-25). Only then does the order to "slay" the opponents come down; thus the execution of 19:27 is best taken to mean not the destruction of Jerusalem by the Romans, but a final destruction of the Jews at the last judgment.

There are two sayings of Jesus in the Gospel that might be taken as exceptions to this general pattern found throughout Luke-Acts in the speeches. They are Luke 19:9, where Jesus declares that "salvation has come" to Zacchaeus, "for he also is a son of Abraham," and 23:34, Jesus' dying prayer that his executioners will be forgiven, "for they do not know what they are doing." Two considerations, however, weigh against concluding that the saying about Zacchaeus is an exception to what Jesus says everywhere else about the Jewish rejection. For one thing, "son of Abraham" is Pauline language for "Christian" (Gal. 3:7), and it could well be that Luke employs that usage at the conclusion of a narrative about the conversion of a toll collector just as he had, a few verses before, employed Pauline language at the conclusion of a parable in which a toll collector proved himself acceptable to God: "justified" (Luke 18:14). Furthermore, when Luke then adds to the phrase "son of Abraham" the declaration that "the Son of man has come to seek and to save what is lost [or 'ruined']" (19:10), he expresses a sentiment that is strongly reminiscent of the attitude displayed in the parable of the banquet. Thus one may be allowed the suspicion that Luke understands Jesus' statement at the conclusion of the Zacchaeus narrative, like the parable of the banquet, to be a reference to the salvation of outcasts as prototypes of Gentiles.[65]

Jesus' forgiveness of his executioners (Luke 23:34),[66] moreover, likewise represents no exception among Jesus' sayings about "the Jews," since it only sets the stage for the mission to the Jews in the first chapters of Acts, which mission is, as we have already seen (Acts 3:17), allowed theologically precisely because of the excuse of ignorance in the execution of Jesus.[67]

Thus Jesus, Peter, Stephen, and Paul present in Luke-Acts, *in what they say on the subject,* an entirely, completely, wholly, uniformly consistent attitude toward the Jewish people as a whole. That attitude is that the Jews are now and always have been willfully ignorant of the purposes and plans of God expressed in their familiar Scriptures, that they always have rejected and will reject God's offer of salvation, that they executed Jesus and persecute and hinder those who try to advance the gospel, and that they get one chance at salvation, which they will of course reject, thus bringing God's wrath down upon them, and quite deservedly so. There is not a single saying, story, or speech put into the mouths of the four leading speakers in Luke-Acts that contradicts this position, and it is repeated over and over in every way possible ad nauseam. Further, we must not forget that Jesus' *first* words at the opening of his public ministry and Paul's *last* words at the close of his are two of the stronger statements of the position. Surely, regarding the *speeches and sayings* in Luke-Acts, Haenchen's judgment is correct without any question: "The theology [of Luke-Acts] . . . no longer sees any sense or any truth in Israel's election . . . Luke has written the Jews off."[68] No divided Israel here.

When we turn to the role of the Jewish people in *the narrative* of Luke-Acts, however, we find quite a different situation, for, in the narrative, the people are often pointedly set apart from their rulers (e.g., Luke 23:35: "The people stood watching, but the rulers mocked."), they "hang on [Jesus'] every word" (Luke 19:48), they grant their favor to the apostles (Acts 2:47), and they both follow Jesus (Luke 12:1) and later are converted to Christianity (Acts 21:20) by the "myriads." Furthermore, Luke frequently writes that Jesus or the apostles are attended by "all the people *(pas ho laos),*" or "the entire people *(ho laos hapas),*" or "the whole people *(holos ho laos).*"[69]

Not only is this description of the behavior of the Jewish people the exact opposite, however, of what is said about them, but the two portraits are often juxtaposed (a characteristic of Luke-Acts that has had much to do with the scholarly consensus about Luke's portrait of the Jews). Thus John the Baptist *says* to the "crowds" that came to him (not just to Pharisees and Sadducees, as in the Matthean parallel) that they are a vile and wicked lot (Luke 3:7-9), but then in the narrative he baptizes "the entire people" (3:21). Likewise, when Jesus begins his public ministry in Nazareth, "*all* attested to him and were amazed at the gracious words that came from his mouth" (4:22), yet Jesus responds with his insult, "You will say . . . , 'Physician, heal yourself,' " and with his analogy from the prophets showing that God's salvation has always been intended for the Gentiles (4:23-27). In 11:29 it is "when the crowds were gathered" that Jesus gives his "this evil generation" speech; and, just following the vicious *saying* of 11:50-51 about the blood of the prophets being required of "this generation," we are told in the narrative that "the crowd" of "myriads" was so great that the people were about "to trample one another" (12:1).

Likewise in the Acts, all three of the announcements of turning to the Gentiles follow hard on what an impartial observer would surely call descriptions of Paul's considerable success among Diaspora Jews and of reasonably good favor from them. In Acts 13:43, "Many of the Jews and of the devout proselytes followed Paul and Barnabas," and Paul and Barnabas "persuaded them to abide in God's grace"; but three verses later Paul condemns the Jews and turns to the Gentiles. To be sure, Jewish opposition has arisen in the two verses in between, but does that opposition entirely erase the success of 13:43? This scenario is repeated exactly, if a little more briefly, in 18:4-6; but the final scene in Acts, where Paul denounces the Roman Jews, does not include the element of Jewish opposition to Paul's preaching. Rather, some of Paul's audience was "persuaded," although others "disbelieved" (28:24); nevertheless, Paul denounces "this people" (28:26) and announces that "this salvation of God has been sent to the Gentiles" (28:28).

How can this enigma be explained? Was Luke-Acts written like an opera, with the composer writing the score and some obscure—and, incidentally, anti-Semitic—librettist writing the speeches to go along with the narrative? Are we, in other words, driven back after all to a redaction theory to explain the present form of Luke-Acts? The disharmonious juxtaposition just sketched would seem to imply such a necessity; yet a closer examination of *plot development* in the narrative of Luke-Acts will show that only one mind is responsible for the narrative and for the speeches, that the apparent disharmonious juxtaposition of the good Jewish people in the narrative and the bad Jewish people in the speeches is quite deliberate and serves a definite purpose, and that our author finally—and quite skillfully, one might add—brings the two together in a successful resolution.[70]

Here, for the sake of space, we must be brief. In the Gospel, up until the passion narrative, the people are distinguished from their leaders, who oppose Jesus, and are represented as responding quite favorably to Jesus. This portrayal of the Jewish people continues into Acts, where they respond as positively to the apostles as they had before to Jesus; and, in addition, Acts reports "myriads" of Jewish conversions to Christianity. The Stephen episode, however, marks a turning point.

Prior to the passion narrative, the narrative of the Gospel represents the Jewish people as being "on Jesus' side."[71] Suddenly, however, and without any explanation whatsoever, when Jesus is brought before Pilate the people are put together with the Jewish religious leaders. After Pilate first examines Jesus, he declares Jesus' innocence to "the chief priests and *the crowds*" (Luke 23:4); yet, when Jesus is taken to Herod, the people disappear, only to be brought back by Pilate for the final hearing, pronunciations of innocence, and deliverance to death. In 23:13 Pilate calls "together the chief priests and the rulers and the people," before whom he twice again pronounces Jesus innocent (23:15,22), but they "cry out as one multitude *(pamplēthei)*" for his death and for the release of Barabbas (23:18, 21, 23). Pilate finally acquiesces and delivers "Jesus to *their* will" (23:25). Here, although Luke has characteristically avoided writing the subjects for the verbs used in the demands for death—so that we read in 23:18 that "*they* cried out," in 23:21 that "*they* shouted," and in 23:23 that "*they* pleaded with loud voices"—"they" nevertheless can be only "the chief priests and the rulers and the people" of 23:13.[72]

After the scenes before Pilate, just as mysteriously, the people are once again set apart from the religious leaders, so that, finally, the strolling companions of the resurrected Jesus on the Emmaus road say (Luke 24:20), "Our chief priests and rulers delivered him and crucified him," thus distancing themselves from the deed. The people do not again appear in opposition until Acts 7. Why do the people appear friendly to Jesus before Luke 23, join the religious leaders in Pilate's presence, and then revert to their friendly status thereafter? To begin with, it is not entirely correct that the people revert to their former status after Luke 23:13. Rather, they take a strangely passive and mute role. When Jesus is led away to be crucified, he is followed by "a great multitude of the people and of women" (23:27), but only the women *(hai)* act like mourners, and Jesus' following warning is addressed only to "daughters of Jerusalem" (23:28-31). At the actual crucifixion, while the religious leaders are mocking, "the people [stand] watching" (23:35)—not doing anything, not mocking, to be sure, but also not mourning, and also not doing anything to prevent the crucifixion, although it is *their* leaders, we must remember, who are carrying out this crucifixion, not the Romans, and although they had, with their rulers, called for Jesus' crucifixion and had thrice heard Pilate pronounce Jesus innocent (Luke 23:4,15,22). Thus Luke seems to want to involve "the people" in guilt for the execution of Jesus while at the same time maintaining the image of the religious leaders as the primary actors.[73] In this, he keeps the people strictly in Pilate's court, where they hear the three findings of innocence, and he keeps them out of Herod's court. Thus the people join with the rulers at the crucial moment; they call for Jesus' death while learning that he is innocent. Have they, then, any excuse? Their beating of their breasts in 23:48 is thus probably to be understood as a recognition of their desperate situation.[74]

When, then, in Luke 24:20 Jesus' interlocutors tell him that *"our* chief priests and rulers" had executed him, it is probably not Luke's intent to absolve "the people" entirely of guilt. For one thing, in Luke 24 the interest has shifted from crucifixion to resurrection, so that Luke is trying to present a scene here in which people who know that Jesus is dead are astounded to find him alive again;[75] but even more—and this is probably the main reason why Jesus' two companions do not say that they had participated in the crucifixion— Luke apparently intends to designate them as Christians, since he has just been narrating how the women have reported the empty tomb to the apostles, and then he writes that "two of *them"* were on the road and encountered Jesus.[76] To be sure, the term "Christian" would be an anachronism here, but Luke is nevertheless describing Jesus' appearances to "his people." Such people, of course, did not execute Jesus.

While the issue of just why the Jewish people appear as they do in Luke 23 and 24 must remain not completely resolved until we come to the end of Acts, still their behavior in Luke is reasonably clear. In the Nazareth episode, the opening of Jesus' public ministry, first *all* in the synagogue respond favorably to Jesus, and then *all* turn against him and seek to kill him. After that, all the people—as opposed to the religious leaders—respond favorably to Jesus up until Luke 23, when they suddenly join with the religious leaders in calling for Jesus' death and in hearing Pilate's acquittals. In the remainder of the Gospel the people only silently observe. One might say that they are in limbo.

The behavior of the Jewish people in the Acts runs parallel to that in the Gospel. Parallels are not, of course, photocopies, so that the behavior of "the Jews" in the Acts is not *exactly* the same as that in the Gospel; nevertheless, there are enough similarities that we can see that Luke was consciously conforming the two narratives to each other in this respect—as, of course, in others.[77] When Acts begins, the Jewish people are, as in the Gospel between the Nazareth episode and the trials before Pilate, uniformly friendly toward and accepting of the apostles. Most obviously, "myriads" (as Acts 21:20 later reminds us) convert. In Acts 6–7, then, Stephen is arrested and killed, a persecution breaks out, and the gospel moves out of Jerusalem on its way to "the end of the earth" (Acts 1:8). And the role of "the Jews" in Acts changes markedly. The most striking evidence of that change is not the response of individual Diaspora synagogues to Paul's ministry, as is often thought, but a shift in the use of the term "the Jews."

Of the 74 certain occurrences of the plural "Jews" or "the Jews" in Luke-Acts, only eight fall before Stephen's martyrdom, of which three occur in the phrase "King of the Jews" in the passion narrative (Luke 23:3, 37, 38). In Luke 7:3 the term is used in a neutral sense to distinguish Jews from Gentiles (the centurion sends "Jewish elders" to Jesus), and in Luke 23:51 it is merely a geographical designation. The other three occurrences are all in Acts 2, where Luke is emphasizing that the first Christian sermon was addressed to Jews native to Jerusalem as well as from elsewhere (Acts 2:5, 10, 14). After Stephen's martyrdom, however, while the neutral use to distinguish Jews from Gentiles still occurs (frequently in Paul's mission, e.g., 14:1, "A great multitude of Jews and of Gentiles"), and while geographical use is still possible (10:39, ". . . in the region of the Jews"), Luke, however, now uses the term "the Jews" *in malam partem* with great frequency.[78] Right away, the first occurrence of the term after Stephen's martyrdom is of this type. In 9:22 Paul "confused the Jews who live in Damascus," and in 9:23 "the Jews conferred together about how to do away with him." This kind of use of "the Jews" continues throughout Acts. Even if many of the instances of "Jews" or "the Jews" after Stephen's martyrdom are of the distinction-from-the-Gentiles type and thus are perhaps natural in that part of the narrative in which the gospel leaves its Jewish matrix, still such usage cannot obscure the fact that, beginning with Acts 9:22, "the Jews" are the enemies of Christianity.

It is often suggested that there is a standard pattern of Jewish response to Paul's ministry, according to which Paul first offers the gospel to Jews but then, after they have rejected it and have turned hostile toward him, pronounces God's judgment on them and turns to the Gentiles. Such a characterization of Jewish response to Paul's mission is not actually correct and, in fact, there is much to be said for the opinion that Luke represents Paul as striving earnestly for Jewish converts;[79] nevertheless, to conclude from that realization, as some do,[80] that Luke intends to give the impression of a mission directed evenhandedly to Jews and Gentiles alike is to miss Luke's point. Rather, he has carefully constructed a progression that is intended to put "the Jews" in a bad light. Skillfully varied as Luke's account of Paul's career is, beginning with the Thessalonian mission (Acts 17) the Lukan Paul *always* goes first to a synagogue when he arrives in town, and he is *always,* except in Athens, opposed by Jews. Inasmuch as Luke in the Athenian episode seems primarily concerned to show in what form the gospel is supposed to be proclaimed when the audience is made up of people with traditional classical educations, perhaps his omission there of the theme of Jewish hostility is understandable; but in Thessalonica (17:5), in Beroea (17:13), in Corinth (18:5-6), and in Ephesus (19:9) Paul is opposed by "the Jews."[81] Thus, for all that Luke has sketched a variegated portrait of Paul's mission, he has also drawn a picture of *increasing Jewish hostility and opposition to the gospel.* The attitude that the Jews in Jerusalem demonstrated *in nuce* in the Stephen affair is therefore revealed in its fullness in historical development in the course of Paul's ministry. The truth of Jewish opposition to the gospel that is announced by Stephen just prior to his being martyred is borne out in a historical progression in the course of Paul's ministry. The accusations are becoming historical reality.[82]

In the Pauline passion narrative,[83] then, the Jewish religious leaders are eclipsed by the people. It is "the Jews" who arrest Paul and who denounce him to the temporal authorities. It is "the whole city" and "the people" (Acts 21:30) who apprehend Paul and the "multitude of the people" (21:36) that demands his death. "They" call for Paul to be "remove[d] from the face of the earth" (22:22), he is brought before the Sanhedrin because he has been "accused by the Jews" (22:30), and it is "the Jews" (23:12) who plot to ambush and kill him. Luke thus makes clear that Paul is done in, not by the religious authorities alone, not by Diaspora Jews alone, and not by Jerusalem alone, but by *THE JEWS*. Jewish opposition to Christianity is now universal and endemic.

When we now turn to Paul's final encounter with Jews at Rome, we shall be able to begin to tie all the threads together. In a sense, Rome is the last stop on Paul's missionary itinerary; it is only that the itinerary has been interrupted by the Passion. As regularly during his mission, and always from the beginning of Acts 17 and on, Paul looks up the Jewish congregation immediately he arrives in town. In this case, of course, since he is in custody, the Jews must come to him, but the setting is otherwise the same; Paul addresses the local Jewish congregation. After they confirm to him what we already know, that Christianity "is everywhere spoken against"—by Jews, apparently—Paul preaches to them, just as regularly during his Diaspora mission; and again, as so frequently there, he "persuades" some, while others "disbelieve" (28:24). Here, however—and in this way this last stop on the itinerary is different from all the others from the beginning of Acts 17 and on—no opposition arises; nevertheless, Paul turns viciously on his auditors, sounding very much like Stephen in quoting Isa. 6:9-10 against them. Then he, for the third and last time, announces that the gospel is going to the Gentiles, "and they will hear" (Acts 28:28).

This final scene of Paul's ministry is therefore a reprise of the first scene of Jesus'.[84] Do we have a synagogue sermon there? So we have here, with the adjustment for verisimilitude that Paul is a prisoner. Is the book of Isaiah quoted there? So it is here. Is there at first a favorable and then a hostile response there? Similarly here the one response is mixed, part favorable and part unfavorable. And does Jesus there make it clear to his audience that they were never the intended recipients of God's salvation, which is a salvation for the Gentiles? So here as well. The issue was never in doubt.[85]

Even the casual reader will realize that I have just gone back on my word. I promised to discuss first what the leading characters in Luke-Acts *said* about the Jewish people, then how the Jewish people *behaved* in the narrative, and finally what relation the two complexes—sayings material and narrative—have with each other. In the last paragraph, however, I seem to have obscured the distinction. I plead guilty to this crime, but I offer this in my defense: it was unavoidable, for the distinction has ceased to exist. At the end of the Acts the Jews have *become* what they from the first *were;* for what Jesus, Stephen, Peter, and Paul say about the Jews—about their intransigent opposition to the purposes of God, about their hostility toward Jesus and the gospel, about their murder of Jesus— is what Luke understands the Jewish people to be in their essence. The narrative shows how existence comes to conform to essence, the process by which the Jewish people become "the Jews"; yet one should not think that the fact that Luke's narrative shows Jews progressing from an attitude of receptivity to one of hostility provides some hope, from Luke's point of view, for Jews; for what they became was no more nor less than what they always, from the days of their creation as a people, were.[86]

Now the behavior of the Jewish people during and after the trial and crucifixion of Jesus is understandable, for there they must fit two stereotypes at once. On the one hand, they must so behave that they deserve the later charge of having murdered Jesus; thus they call for Jesus' death and hear Pilate's acquittals. But, on the other hand, they must also so behave that the possibility of mass conversions in Acts 1–5 is a real possibility; thus they follow Jesus mutely to the cross, stand passively at the side while their leaders kill him, and beat their breasts when he dies. By giving the Jewish people such a strange role in the passion, Luke has prepared the way for both necessities in Acts, that of the success of the gospel among "the Jews" and that of their rejection of the gospel. If Luke had constructed his script so that the people entered completely the mode of rejection at the end of the Gospel, then the narrative of the Acts would have been anticlimactic,[87] but if they expressed no hostility to the purposes of God during the passion narrative, then the absolute reality expressed in the sayings and speeches from the

Nazareth episode and on would not be correct. So Luke gives to the Jewish people the ambiguous role in the passion narrative already described. When they then take an active and quite unambiguous role in the Pauline passion narrative, we see better where the passion narrative of the Gospel was heading. The true role of the Jewish people is prefigured in the Nazareth episode, where Jesus' audience turns with one accord against him. "Luke made it clear that neither Jesus nor his followers had rejected the Jews; they had excluded themselves from the Christian community."[88] In the passion narrative, then, in the martyrdom of Stephen, and finally in the Pauline passion narrative, they become by stages what the Nazareth episode had already shown us they were.[89] Thus Luke shows by a *historical progression* (Haenchen) the correctness of Jesus' statement that "the blood of all the prophets" will "be required of this generation" (Luke 11:50); of Stephen's statement that the Jewish ancestors "killed those who proclaimed beforehand the coming of the Righteous One, whose deliverers and murderers now [the Jews] have become" (Acts 7:52); and of Paul's statement that the Jews' "blood" will "be upon [their] head" (Acts 18:6).[90] The familiar epochal plan of Luke-Acts—which has been recognized, in one form or another, almost since the beginning of critical New Testament scholarship and which Conzelmann has especially emphasized—is but a means to an end. It is Luke's way of describing becoming, becoming culminating in being, being that is already present from the beginning in the sayings and speeches.

As a last consideration, the differences that have emerged between my work and that of Robert Tannehill in our published studies of Luke-Acts are worth noting. On the one hand, Tannehill sees just as clearly as I do that Luke has portrayed the Jews as totally rejecting Jesus, the church, and the message of salvation and as thereby bringing on themselves God's condemnation and punishment. Some years ago he wrote, in an analysis of Luke 4:16-30,

> It should not be surprising that the scene which Luke places at the beginning of the ministry of Jesus also serves to interpret the development which follows it. It does so by announcing that it is not those who are closest to Jesus but others who will benefit from his work, and by establishing the pattern of rejection by Jesus' own people and moving on to others which will be typical of the mission as a whole.

It also does so by interpreting the whole mission of Jesus through the Isaiah quotation. The significance of this quotation is not limited to the particular situation in Nazareth. *It is the title under which Luke places the whole ministry of Jesus* and is to be understood as a summary of Jesus' work and message throughout Luke's gospel.[91]

More recently, however, Tannehill has argued that Luke portrays this two-sided rejection of the Jews as a *tragedy*. According to this interpretation, the accelerating theme of Jewish rejection after Stephen's martyrdom is a tragic turn in the narrative; thus Luke intended for his readers to view the Jews with "sympathetic pity."[92] While I would like to agree with this position, I cannot, for a reason that Tannehill has himself noted, and that is that the tragedy in Luke-Acts obviously lies elsewhere. Tannehill writes that Luke guides his "readers to experience the story of Israel *and its messiah* as a tragic story."[93] Are we to think that Luke-Acts is a double tragedy? Surely not! The tragedy of the Gospel is the execution of the Last Great Prophet, who journeys through the pages of the Gospel toward his inescapable fate. "The Jews" are the villains, not the victims.[94]

5

INSIDER OR OUTSIDER? LUKE'S RELATIONSHIP WITH JUDAISM

Marilyn Salmon

In his discussion of scholarship on the portrayal of the Jews in Luke-Acts, Jack T. Sanders expresses amazement that the representatives of such divergent views could actually have read the same edition of Luke-Acts. That sentiment is appropriate to the situation. How can the same text yield the different interpretations represented by the articles in this volume? Could we really have read the same edition of the text?

Why is it that the text yields such divergent results? The answer, I think, is context. In what context do we place the text? More specifically, and more to the point of this particular discussion, how do we understand the author's relationship with Judaism? Is the writer of Luke-Acts an insider or an outsider? Does he stand outside Judaism or is he *mishpahah*? Does he identify himself as a Jew, or not? How we define the author in terms of his relationship to Judaism determines how we read the text.

I know that Sanders and I have read the same text. His paper reveals a careful and thoughtful reading of the text. By any standard, he presents a clearly defined method and a well-argued case that Luke regards the Jewish people as a whole as universally and endemically opposed to Christianity. The Jews, in his narrative, are the villains. I disagree with that conclusion, however. The reason why I disagree with this interpretation of the text is that I do not share Sanders' perception of Luke as an outsider. While Sanders does not actually say that Luke is an outsider, in his view Luke is not a Jew by his own or anyone else's definition. I think that this view informs the way Sanders reads the text.

The question posed at the beginning of his article implies that Sanders perceives Luke as an outsider: "What, exactly, does Luke think of the Jewish people as a whole, of 'the Jews'?" He later acknowledges a more neutral question, namely, whether Luke thinks of them as a collective entity. But the question Sanders pursues is the initial one: What does Luke think of the Jewish people as a whole? If Luke is indeed an outsider, he might very well have an opinion of the Jews, collectively, as a whole people. But that is the perspective of an outsider. Outsiders form opinions of people collectively, as a whole, what they are in their essence, whether it is "the Jews" or "the Blacks" or "Catholics" or "women." But that is not the perspective of an insider. We do not have that distance from groups in which we are included or by self-definition identify ourselves. The problem is, of course, that sometimes insiders and outsiders use the same, or similar words in describing a particular group. So, in order to know what the words mean, we must first know the perspective of the speaker. This is especially true when the words are critical or harsh, because self-criticism differs from external criticism in meaning, intent, in the ways it is heard and interpreted. Spoken from the outside, harsh words are condemning; from the inside, the same words are prophetic. For example, Sanders quotes Stephen's speech in Acts:

> Hard-necked and uncircumcised in hearts and ears, you always thrust against the Holy Spirit; as your fathers, so you. Whom of the prophets did your fathers not persecute? And they killed those who proclaimed beforehand the coming of the Righteous One, whose deliverers and murderers now you have become, you who received the Law in angelic ordinances; and you did not keep it. (7:51-53)

Sanders classifies this passage as evidence of the blanket condemnation variety, "according to which Jews are by nature and congenitally obstreperous and opposed to the will and purposes of God and have been, as a group and as a nation, excluded from God's salvation."[1] Concerning the same text, David L. Tiede observes that "there is nothing anti-Jewish or foreign to Jewish tradition in such an indictment. The prophetic heritage long before taught how Israel's history could be recited against her."[2] If Luke is an outsider, then I think Sanders' conclusion is correct. If Luke is an insider, then these words are not rightly understood as a blanket condemnation of the Jewish people as a whole, but rather, as Tiede concludes, prophetic, with the intent to effect change.

Sanders understands Luke's audience to be outsiders as well, and this perspective, too, leads to a particular reading of the text. For example, in describing how Luke builds the image of general Jewish guilt in chap. 10 of the Gospel by omitting subjects for the verbs rather than indicting Jewish leaders, he concludes: "Since he [Luke] had just written that Jesus worked among the Jews, what is the Gentile reader to think but that 'the Jews' killed Jesus?"[3] But what if the readers are not Gentiles? If they are not, then Luke is not necessarily building an image of general Jewish guilt. He may be omitting what he does not need to say. Insiders would know which Jews he was implicating. On another occasion, Sanders observes:

> Even if many of the instances of "Jews" or "the Jews" after Stephen's martyrdom are of the distinction-from-the-Gentiles type and thus are perhaps natural in that part of the narrative in which the gospel leaves its Jewish matrix, still such usage cannot obscure the fact that, beginning with Acts 9:22, "the Jews" are the enemies of Christianity.[4]

I do not understand where "the gospel leaves its Jewish matrix." I do not think that it does in Luke-Acts. That observation notwithstanding, in terms of what Luke is saying to his audience, whether the distinction between Jew and Gentile is natural or neutral depends on the perspective of audience and author. Further, that the Jews are the enemies of Christianity could be regarded as a fact only if one assumes, first, that Luke is not a Jew and, second, that Christianity is a religion separate from Judaism and that Jews who are Christians are not Jews. Apart from these suppositions, the text may not support this interpretation.

It is thus a critical question to ask where Luke stands with respect to Judaism. Is he an insider or an outsider? How one answers that question determines how one reads the text.

Does the text commend one view more than the other? Or does appealing to the text for evidence merely engage us in circular reasoning? The danger of circular reasoning is present, but it seems that the logical and only thing to do is to look at the text for clues as to the author's relationship with Judaism. For the following reasons, I think Luke perceives himself to be a Jew.

First, Luke makes distinctions among Jews, and he distinguishes on many levels. He knows a Pharisee from a Sadducee. That is hardly conclusive evidence that he is an insider. Any casual observer could make that distinction, but it is worth asking why a non-Jew, knowing nothing of Palestinian affairs and writing after the fall of the temple when Sadducees were presumably extinct, would be interested in the distinction and supposed implications for the Christian movement. Luke knows of believing Jews and nonbelieving Jews. It does not take an insider to make that distinction, but I do wonder if or why an outsider would be interested in narrating the successes of the mission, small and great, among Jews, even to the end of the narrative where Paul persuades some in the synagogue in Rome.

Luke also distinguishes between believing and nonbelieving Pharisees.[5] I think it is significant that Luke distinguishes one Pharisee from another. It seems to me that making distinctions among members of a group within a religious group reflects the interest and awareness of an insider more than an outsider. It also suggests that, in Luke's view, one does not stop being a Jew by virtue of becoming a believer or, as we would say, a Christian.

Second, Luke gives a great deal of attention to Torah observance. His heroes, Jesus in the Gospel, Paul in Acts, are observant Jews. Jesus, who was circumcised in accordance with Torah, frequents the synagogue and teaches there. In controversies involving Sabbath observance, Luke portrays Jesus as acting in accordance with the Law.[6] The Paul of Acts is the model Pharisee.[7] Gentile Christians are exempt only from circumcision in their observance of Torah. There are no exemptions for Jews.[8] These are but a few examples of this interest.[9] A plausible explanation for this attention is that this concern reflects the perspective of an insider, a Torah-observant Christian Jew. An insider would more likely be concerned about such matters than an outsider, especially one with a low opinion of the Jewish people as a whole.

Third, no one would disagree that the Gentile mission is a prominent theme in Acts, and probably the Gospel as well. It has typically been taken for granted that this fact implies that Luke and his audience are Gentiles. I think the prominence of this theme and Luke's interest in Gentiles supports just the opposite conclusion. "Gentile" means "not Jewish." The designation itself reflects a Jewish perspective of the world. People who are not Jewish do not normally think of themselves in that way, as not Jewish, unless, of course, they are a minority among Jews. In that context they might identify themselves in terms of what they are not. "Gentile" is a label Jews use to designate anyone who is not a Jew. "Gentile" is Jewish for "outsider." I think Christians frequently identify with the Gentiles in reading the New Testament, reading "Gentile" as a synonym for "Christian." This interpretation misses the point that the term "Gentile" is relevant within Judaism. Once we move outside a Jewish matrix to a situation where the church is predominantly non-Jewish, the label "not Jewish" is irrelevant. It is relevant to Luke, however, and I think that this relevance suggests that he views the world from a Jewish perspective.

Fourth, Luke refers to the Christian movement as a *hairesis,* the same term that he and Josephus[10] use for the constituent parties, or sects, within Judaism. In Acts 15:5, for example, Luke mentions believers who belong to the *hairesis* of the Pharisees. According to Acts 24:5 and 28:22, nonbelieving Jews identify the Christian movement as a *hairesis,* and Paul defends this *hairesis* on the grounds that it does not in any way deviate from the Law and the prophets (24:14-16). If Luke is merely recording historical fact, this textual clue may not be relevant here, but if in relating the past he is revealing something of his own situation—and I believe that he is—then his use of *hairesis* suggests that he considers himself an insider.

I cannot prove that Luke is an insider, but I am persuaded by these clues from the text that he believes that he stands within Judaism.

Luke does, nevertheless, say some very uncomplimentary things about Jews. According to Sanders, the speeches in Luke-Acts are entirely consistent in condemning the Jews, without qualification, with no distinctions made. Indeed, the words are harsh, critical, condemning. But what do the words mean? Sanders writes,

What Jesus, Stephen, Peter, and Paul say about the Jews—about their intransigent opposition to the purposes of God, about their hostility toward Jesus and the gospel, about their murder of Jesus—is what Luke understands the Jewish people to be in their essence.[11]

The condemning words in the speeches reflect what Luke thinks of the Jewish people as a whole, collectively. I disagree. I think these harsh words reflect Luke's view toward Jews who have not accepted the gospel—not all Jews—even though he does not say so explicitly. Luke does distinguish among Jews in the narrative, and that is precisely Sanders' point—in the *narrative*. In his reading of the text, though, the narrative in the end conforms to the speeches. The people become, in the narrative, what they always were in the speeches.[12] I give the distinctions in the narrative more weight, however, not least of all because I am not convinced that after Acts 9:22 the Jews are uniformly enemies of Christianity. In Acts 13:42-43, "many Jews and devout converts to Judaism" urge Paul and Barnabas to continue their preaching. In 14:1-2 Jews are included among those who believed, and it is specifically "unbelieving Jews" who stir up the non-Jews. Some are persuaded in Thessalonica (17:4), and in Beroea noble Jews receive the word with eagerness, and many believed (17:11-12). Paul persuades Jews at Corinth (18:4), and Jews at Ephesus urge him to stay (18:20). At the end of the narrative Paul convinces some in Rome, and there is disagreement among them (28:24-25). The distinction Luke makes is not between Jew and non-Jew. His distinction is between believing Jew and nonbelieving Jew. All are Jews.

Further, the speeches which appear to be so condemning are given by Jews. Of course, this would be meaningless if Luke disassociated his heroes from their Jewishness. But he does not. His heroes are not incidentally Jewish due to an accident of birth. Their Jewishness is not in their past. They are Jews—exemplary, pious, Torah-observant Jews. Luke does not have to portray them that way, but he seems to be quite self-conscious in doing so. In addition to these Jews who give major speeches, Luke emphasizes the piety of other Jews whom he names: Gamaliel, who gives a short but moving speech in defense of the apostles, Joseph of Arimathea, and Elizabeth, Zechariah, Mary, Joseph, Simeon, and Anna. Could he really be holding up these Jews as exemplary in their faithfulness to Torah, on the one hand, while at the same time including them in a categorical condemnation of the Jewish people as a whole?

Also there are the believing Jews—we would call them Christians, though Luke does not—other than the named ones. Could Luke really mean to condemn believing Jews along with nonbelieving

Jews for the murder of Jesus, for rejecting the will of God? If we conclude that the speeches tell us what Luke thinks of the Jewish people as a whole, what they are in their essence, then they are necessarily included, unless Jews who are Christians are not Jews, a view inconsistent with the text.

I can conclude only that Luke does not mean to implicate all Jews when he condemns "the Jews." The obvious question is, of course: if he did not mean the Jews, all the Jews, then why did he not say so? I think he did not say so because he did not need to say so. It would have been obvious to him and to his audience which Jews he meant. They knew which Jews were guilty. We put too great a burden on our narrator to expect him to clarify for outsiders what is obvious to insiders. And it is not entirely beside the point to add that the judgment of guilt is determined by insiders, not outsiders.

I disagree with the conclusions of Sanders' essay, not because I find weaknesses in his method or in the logic of his argument, but because I do not share his definition of Luke's relationship with Judaism. If Sanders is right, that Luke is an outsider, then his interpretation of the text is correct. If Luke's perspective is that of an insider, then we must read the text differently. How we define the author in terms of first-century Judaism determines how we read Luke-Acts.

6
REJECTION BY JEWS AND TURNING TO GENTILES: THE PATTERN OF PAUL'S MISSION IN ACTS

Robert C. Tannehill

Paul's announcements in Acts that he is turning to the Gentiles in response to Jewish rejection have strongly influenced scholarly assessment of the Lukan attitude toward Judaism. It will be useful to take a new look at these announcements in their contexts.[1]

ANTIOCH

Following Paul's speech in Antioch of Pisidia, Paul and Barnabas encounter Jewish opposition and solemnly declare that they are turning to the Gentiles (Acts 13:46). Awareness of the rest of the narrative should lead us to eliminate certain interpretations of this event that might otherwise be advanced. The announcement cannot mean that Paul will never again preach to Jews, for as soon as he reaches the next town, he begins his mission by preaching in the synagogue to Jews (14:1). He preaches to Jews repeatedly in his continuing mission. Paul's announcement also cannot mean that Gentiles are offered the word of God only because of Jewish rejection, as an afterthought or as a second choice. The narrator of Luke-Acts has made clear ever since the birth narrative that the purpose of God which shapes this story intends to work salvation for all peoples. This was announced by an inspired prophet (Luke 2:30-32) and proclaimed as God's purpose in a banner quotation of Scripture (Luke 3:6). Then an inclusive mission of preaching was entrusted by the risen Messiah to his apostles (Luke 24:47; Acts 1:8). Preaching to the Gentiles is part of God's saving purpose announced long ago in Scripture, and it is a task entrusted by the risen Messiah to his witnesses. It is also part of the commission that Paul received from the risen Lord, governing his ministry (Acts 9:15; 22:15; 26:16-18). It is not an afterthought, nor does it need to be justified by Jewish rejection. In the narrator's view, salvation for the Gentiles is firmly rooted in Scripture, the witness to God's ancient purpose, as the Antioch scene also makes clear. In Acts 13:47 Paul and Barnabas quote from Scripture a command of the Lord which governs their ministry, obligating them to bring light to the nations and salvation "to the end of the earth" (heōs eschatou tēs gēs, as in the command to the apostles in 1:8).

In order to understand why turning to the Gentiles is nevertheless a special event which deserves a dramatic announcement, we must consider the first part of the declaration in Antioch: "To you it was necessary that the word of God be spoken first" (13:46). The mission is universal, but it must follow a prescribed order. The Jews must be addressed first. If they reject the gospel, the missionaries are free to begin the second phase of their mission. But why was it "necessary" that the preachers speak to the Jews "first"?

The message that Paul delivered in the Antioch synagogue provides some clues. In order to appreciate the narrator's perspective, it is important to keep the complete Antioch episode in mind, giving full weight both to the synagogue speech and to the announcement on the following Sabbath, for the poignancy of the announcement depends on the content of the synagogue speech. Interpretation that forgets the speech when interpreting the announcement will miss the unresolved tension in the narrator's attitude toward unbelieving Jews, a tension to which the total scene gives powerful expression.

Not only the setting but also the content makes clear that this is a speech by a Jew to Jews, for it concerns God's promise to the Jewish people. Paul addresses his audience as "Israelites" and "sons of the family of Abraham" (13:16,26). He also stresses his own position in this family by calling his audience "brothers" (13:26,

38). The speech is addressed to this particular people and those who have chosen to associate with it ("those who fear God," 13:16,26). The review of Israel's history at the beginning of the speech is more than a "reference to the depicted situation," a repeated feature of the mission speeches in Acts.[2] This introduction to the speech affirms the election of Israel (13:17) and God's faithful care for the elect people. The raising up of David as king and the promise concerning his offspring continue this faithful care. Once David is mentioned, the speech focuses on him and his promised heir. The speech is basically the announcement, with supporting argument, that the promised heir has come and has been installed as Messiah through resurrection. The turning point of the speech is 13:23, where, following statements that almost any Jew would accept, Paul announces something new: the promise has now been fulfilled through Jesus. The word "promise" *(epangelia)* in this verse becomes a theme word when it reappears in 13:32-33 in a more forceful proclamation of the fulfillment of the promise. The narrative concerning Jesus (13:27-31) leads up to this proclamation that the promise has been fulfilled through Jesus' resurrection, and 13:33b-39 develops the significance of this event through Scripture and an invitation to forgiveness. Thus the fulfillment of the promise to Israel of an heir to David's throne is the leading idea of the speech.[3]

After announcing that Jesus is the promised "Savior" from David's line (13:23),[4] Paul emphasizes the special importance of this announcement for his Jewish audience: "To us[5] the word of this salvation has been sent out" (13:26). The placement of the personal pronoun in initial position in the clause indicates the stress. When Paul again relates his message to his audience in 13:32-33, the stress on the special significance of this message for the Jewish people reappears. He is announcing the fulfillment of the promise made to their fathers concerning a king for Israel.

Paul in 13:32-33 is speaking of the promised king of David's line, as is shown by the further references to David in 13:34,36, and by the close connection of this section of Paul's sermon to Peter's Pentecost sermon. The reference to Ps. 16:10 (15:10 LXX) in 13:35-37 is a brief reminder of the more extensive quotation and application of this psalm in Acts 2:25-31. There Peter argued that David was not speaking of himself but of his descendant, concerning whom God had sworn an oath to seat him on David's throne (2:30). It is

Jesus, risen and seated at God's right hand, who fulfills this promise. The oath of which Peter spoke is equivalent to the promise of which Paul speaks; both refer to the expected Davidic king for Israel. Peter connected the resurrection of Jesus to the oath that God would seat David's descendant on David's throne and proclaimed Jesus, seated at God's right hand, as the promised Lord and Messiah. Similarly, Paul proclaims God's resurrection of Jesus (*anastēsas Iēsoun*, 13:33) as the fulfillment of the messianic promise. Through resurrection and exaltation[6] Jesus is declared to be God's Son, which is equivalent to the enthronement mentioned in 2:30. The context strongly supports the view that 13:33 refers to Jesus' resurrection as the fulfillment of the messianic promise, for Jesus' resurrection is the subject throughout 13:30-37.[7]

The messianic significance of Jesus' resurrection is developed through the scriptural quotations in 13:34-35.[8] There Paul indicates that the risen one is "no longer going to return to corruption." This places emphasis on continuing freedom from death, an emphasis that is supported by reference to "the holy things of David which are faithful," i.e., lasting.[9] The emphasis in 13:34 fits well with the description of the Messiah in the angel's announcement to Mary. He will not only be called God's Son and receive "the throne of David his father." He will also "reign over the house of Jacob forever, and of his kingdom there will be no end" (Luke 1:32-33).[10] Since the Messiah has been enthroned through resurrection, he is no longer threatened by corruption, and his kingdom will have no end.

The significance of this messianic promise for the Jewish people is expressed by the quotation of Isa. 55:3 in Acts 13:34, a quotation which usually receives too little attention. The plural pronoun *hymin* shows that this promise is not a promise to the Messiah but to the Jewish people (in the context of the speech, to Paul's audience). The application of Paul's message to his audience is strongly stressed through first or second person plural pronouns, sometimes in emphatic position, in 13:26,32,33,38. The pronoun in the quotation in 13:34 fits with these other pronouns and refers to the same group. Since the verb in the quotation has been changed from the verb in Isa. 55:3 LXX and the pronoun is the indirect object of that verb, it could easily have been changed if it did not serve the narrator's purpose. Instead, the pronoun has been allowed to stand. Paul through this quotation affirms the promise of the messianic kingdom for the Jewish people and again acknowledges that this promise is firmly rooted in Scripture.

The verb in the Isaiah quotation has been changed so as to match the verb in the psalm quotation that follows. The words which these two quotations have in common, as well as the way that they are introduced, indicate that they are to be interpreted together. Indeed, they are understood to be the positive and negative expression of the same basic promise, and the parts correspond: "I will give to you" / "You will not give"; "the holy things of David" / "your holy one"; "which are faithful" / "to see corruption." The connection between the last two phrases, which is not apparent in the wording, is established by the introduction to the Isaiah quotation in 13:34: the messianic kingdom is "faithful" because the risen Messiah is "no longer going to return to corruption" but will rule over an eternal kingdom. The reference to "the holy things of David" helps to make clear that "your holy one" refers to the Davidic Messiah. While the strange phrase *ta hosia Dauid* is open to several interpretations, the reference to something belonging to David in a promise applying to people of Paul's time naturally calls to mind the promised kingdom of David's heir, especially after 13:22-23, 32-33.[11]

The Antioch scene repeats themes from both of Peter's first two speeches, an example of the common Lukan practice of sounding important themes more than once. The Pentecost speech helps us to understand Paul's reference to Jesus' resurrection as the fulfillment of God's oath to David. The speech in Solomon's portico helps us to understand the necessity of Paul's speaking first to the Jews (see 13:46). After making clear that God will still send the "times of refreshment" and "restoration" associated with the Messiah if the people of Jerusalem repent (3:19-21), Peter ends his second speech by saying, "God, having raised up his servant, sent him to you first" (3:26). This is explained by the preceding reference to his hearers as "sons of the prophets and of the covenant which God covenanted with our fathers" (3:25). The covenantal promise is described as a blessing that "all the families of the earth" will share, but it is clear that the Jewish people are meant to share in this blessing as "first" (3:25-26). The way that this priority is highlighted in Acts and its connection with the Jewish people as "sons of the prophets and of the covenant" show that the narrator still understands the scriptural promises quite concretely as promises to the Jewish people, even though Jewish Scripture also promises salvation for all nations. The narrator affirms God's promise to the Jewish people found in Scripture and is therefore willing to have one of his chief characters say that God sent his servant "to you first." This determines the course of the mission. If God sent the risen Messiah and his blessings to the Jews first, in fulfillment of promises to their ancestors, Paul must speak to the Jews first, as he indicates in 13:46.

The risen Messiah's instructions to his apostles also recognize this. The extension of the mission to the Gentiles is clearly stated in the two versions of the commission to the apostles, but both also indicate where the mission must begin: in Jerusalem, the center of Jewish life (Luke 24:47; Acts 1:4,8).

The preceding discussion should make clear that the narrator of Acts is not merely giving a Jewish coloring to Paul's Antioch speech to make it fit the synagogue setting. Paul's preaching reflects a view that characterizes Luke-Acts from its beginning, the view that Jesus is the Davidic Messiah who fulfills specific promises of God to the Jewish people. These promises are found in Scripture, which the narrator accepts as the revelation of God's saving purpose for Israel and the world. To assume that Jewish rejection will permanently block the fulfillment of these promises for the synagogue audiences addressed by Paul is to assume that a major aspect of God's saving purpose can be defeated. This defeat would not be complete, perhaps, for Acts affirms the success of the mission among some Jews, especially in Jerusalem. But Acts also makes us aware that the mission is not successful among many Jews; indeed, the sequel to Paul's Antioch sermon will highlight Jewish rejection. The Antioch sermon views Israel from the viewpoint of God's saving purpose and scriptural promise. The theological problem is how that purpose and promise can remain valid in the face of Jewish rejection. In my opinion, this is a problem that Acts never resolves. Nevertheless, it does not mitigate the problem and reduce the tension by weakening the witness to God's saving purpose and scriptural promise to the Jewish people. Apparently, living with the tension is preferable to ignoring either of two fundamental realities: God's promise to Israel, fulfilled in Jesus, and Israel's rejection.

Furthermore, Paul's sermon at Antioch is the primary place where the narrator reveals the content of Paul's mission preaching to Jews.

The later brief summaries of Paul's preaching to Jews are to be understood in light of this fuller statement. This sermon, then, has a key role in indicating the place of Israel in Paul's gospel, according to Acts.

What, then, of the announcement in 13:46 that, since the Jews are rejecting the word of God, Paul and Barnabas are turning to the Gentiles? Several aspects of the context need to be noted to help us understand more clearly what is happening. First, Paul began by speaking in the synagogue to the Jewish assembly. Turning to the Gentiles means the end of such preaching in the Antioch synagogue. Second, the situation changes because Jews "were contradicting the things being said by Paul, reviling them" (or "blaspheming" the Lord Jesus; the object of *blasphēmountes* is not specified). Resistance is openly expressed and involves personal attacks that would make continued preaching in the synagogue difficult or impossible. Third, when they are thrown out, Paul and Barnabas shake off the dust from their feet and go to another city. In doing this, they are following the instructions Jesus gave to the 12 and the 72 (Luke 9:5; 10:11), instructions that apply when a *city* fails to receive the mission. The context in Acts 13:51 is the same, for this gesture is used as the missionaries leave one city and go to another, where the mission to the Jews will begin again. So the announcement of turning to the Gentiles applies first of all to the city of Antioch. Of course, we must also note that the narrator has given a great deal of space to what happened at Antioch, suggesting that it may have special importance for understanding Paul's mission.

CORINTH, EPHESUS, AND JERUSALEM

It is widely recognized that the announcement of turning to the Gentiles in Antioch is the first of a series of similar scenes in Acts. These are often reckoned to be three in number,[12] although there are several additional scenes that should be noted. The second of these scenes, set in Corinth (18:5-6), will help us to clarify the understanding of Paul's mission to Jews and Gentiles. The sequence of events begins with Paul "testifying to the Jews that the Messiah is Jesus." This summary recalls an important aspect of Paul's message as previously presented in the Antioch synagogue. In the next verse Paul announces, "From now on I will go to the Gentiles." The cause of the announcement closely parallels the situation in Antioch. The announcement is made when the Jews are "resisting and reviling" (or "blaspheming"). Paul shakes out his garments as he makes his announcement, a gesture that parallels the shaking off of dust from the feet in 13:51. However, this gesture has a slightly different meaning here, for it does not take place as Paul leaves the city. Indeed, a vision of the Lord makes clear that Paul is to stay in this city (18:9-11). But the announcement and gesture are still accompanied by a change of location. Paul has been preaching in the synagogue (18:4). When he begins to encounter strong resistance, he transfers to the house of Titius Justus (18:7). The practical effect of Paul's gesture and announcement is that Paul no longer uses the synagogue as his place of preaching. Paul's announcement indicates a shift from a synagogue-based mission, addressed to Jews and to those Gentiles attracted to Judaism, to a mission in the city at large, where the population is predominantly Gentile. The narrator makes clear that Paul's mission to Jews and Godfearers had some success, mentioning Titius Justus (who presumably has become a believer, since he offers his house for Paul's use) and Crispus, a synagogue ruler, who "believed the Lord with all his house" (18:7-8).

Paul's announcement in 18:6 includes the words, "Your blood is [or 'will be'] on your head; I am clean." These words are to be understood in light of the necessity laid on Paul to speak the word of God first to the Jews, as stated in 13:46. References to blood-guilt as responsibility for someone else's death, as in Matt. 23:35; 27:25; Acts 5:28, are not close parallels, for here the Corinthian Jews are responsible for their own blood. *They* are responsible, not Paul, as he emphasizes with the statement, "I am clean." The situation is like that of the prophetic "watchman" described in Ezek. 33:1-9, and Paul borrows the language of Ezek. 33:4 *(to haima autou epi tēs kephalēs autou estai)*. The watchman is one who hears a word from God and is obligated to speak it to the people. If he does not, the blood of those who perish will be demanded from the hand of the watchman; if he does, the blood of those who perish will be on their own heads. Paul is declaring that he has fulfilled his obligation to speak God's word to God's people.[13] They are now responsible for their own fate. The pattern of speaking first to Jews and only later turning to the Gentiles testifies to Paul's sense of prophetic obligation to his own people. He is released from this obligation only when he meets strong public resistance within the Jewish community. Then he can begin the second phase of his mission within a city, a phase in which the conversion of individual Jews is still possible, although Paul is no longer preaching in the synagogue or addressing Jews as a community.

In Acts 19:8-10 (Ephesus) there is no announcement by Paul that he is turning to the Gentiles, but we are told of a shift from the synagogue to the school of Tyrannus as the location of Paul's work. The circumstances are similar to the texts previously discussed. The change takes place when "some were becoming hardened and were disbelieving, speaking evil *(kakologountes)* of the way before the multitude" (19:9). Note that these attitudes and actions are attributed only to "some" *(tines)*. Nevertheless, Paul ends his preaching and discussing in the synagogue. While it comes from only some of the Jews, the opposition is vocal and public. It could include heckling and disruption of the assembly. Under these circumstances Paul moves his mission to another setting. Indeed, we are told that he not only withdrew but also "separated the disciples" (19:9). This remark suggests permanent consequences to the shift of mission locations in response to Jewish rejection: Christian disciples are becoming a separate religious community. The repeated references to resistance in the synagogue, followed by a shift to a Gentile location, suggest that the narrator is adjusting to a hard fact. The Christian message belongs in the synagogue, since it is first of all a message to Jews about their Messiah, but, under the circumstances, the synagogue cannot be a place of Christian preaching.

We have now observed that on three occasions (13:45-46; 18:4-7; 19:8-9) a shift from the synagogue to another location for preaching is the result of "reviling" (or "blaspheming") and "speaking evil" by Jews. Two of the announcements that Paul is turning to the Gentiles are found in these settings, indicating that they announce a shift from a synagogue-based mission to a mission at large because public opposition by Jews no longer allows preaching in the synagogue.

At the end of his first imprisonment speech, Paul reports a message which he received from the Lord during his first preaching in Jerusalem. The Lord commanded Paul to leave Jerusalem, since "they will not receive your witness about me," and go "to nations [or 'Gentiles'] afar" (22:18,21). Here we have the same pattern: Jewish refusal leads to a mission among the Gentiles. To be sure, there are also differences: Paul does not announce what he is going to do; he is commanded by the Lord. Paul even seems to protest when the Lord orders him to leave. Paul is portrayed as reluctant to abandon his mission in Jerusalem.

The story implies, of course, that the Lord knows better. Paul here begins to learn how things will frequently go in his preaching: Jews will often reject his witness, and he should then turn to the Gentiles. This pattern of mission, which is here traced back to a command of the Lord, is presented in a simplified way. Paul does not preach only to Gentiles when he leaves Jerusalem. He repeatedly begins by preaching to Jews. In this temple vision the many experiences of Jewish rejection and continuation of the mission in a Gentile setting are reduced to a single movement: from Jerusalem into the Gentile world. But the vision scene also maintains a symbolic contact with Judaism (it takes place in the temple) and expresses Paul's reluctance to abandon his mission in Jerusalem. The temple location may hint at the irony of the situation: Jews are rejecting a message that originates from the core of their own faith. It may also recall Isaiah's temple vision (Isa. 6:1-8), a prophetic call that leads directly into the bitter message that Paul will quote in 28:26-27 (= Isa. 6:9-10), although the indications of this connection to Isaiah's vision are not very clear.

Acts 22:17-21 does not provide a setting for the Lord's command by reporting actual resistance to Paul's witness. However, the narrator's understanding of the situation is indicated by the earlier report of Paul's preaching in Jerusalem in 9:29-30. Paul left Jerusalem, we are told, because of a plot against his life. "The brothers" learned about this and "sent him out" to Tarsus. The *exapesteilan* in 9:30 apparently describes the human execution of what is presented in 22:21 as the Lord's command *(exapostelō)*.

ROME

The final scene to which we must give some detailed attention presents Paul speaking to the Jews in Rome. Since this is the last major scene in Acts, followed only by a brief two-verse summary of Paul's continuing preaching, it has special importance. The final scene of a narrative is an opportunity to clarify central aspects of plot and characterization in the preceding story and to make a final, lasting impression on the readers. The fact that the narrator has chosen to end the work with a scene which focuses on Paul's encounter with Jews shows how extraordinarily important the issues of this encounter are to the narrator. We must recognize, however, that this final scene of Acts is actually a double scene (28:17-22,23-28), in which Paul makes two important statements to the Roman Jews. When we acknowledge the importance of both of these statements and allow them to resonate against each other, we will see that Acts' portrait of Paul in relation to Israel is richer and more complex than often thought.

Paul's statement in 28:17-20 is a summary of the preceding trial narrative and imprisonment speeches in Acts 22–26. It presents what the narrator most wants readers to retain from that long narrative. Paul claims that he was recognized as innocent of any serious crime when examined by the Romans (28:18; cf. 23:28-29; 25:25; 26:31-32). Primary emphasis falls, however, on Paul's claim that he has "done nothing opposed to the people or the customs received from the fathers" (28:17). Such charges were made in 21:21,28; 24:5-6, and Paul previously denied them in 25:8,10. He also assures the Roman Jews that in his appeal to Caesar he does not intend to bring an accusation against his own nation (28:19). Thus considerable stress is placed on Paul's loyalty to Israel and its way of life.[14] In 28:17 Paul is not merely saying that he is a loyal Jew like many others. He is asserting that his mission has not been an anti-Jewish movement. Furthermore, he remains loyal to his people in spite of the opposition which he has experienced from many of his fellow Jews. Indeed, he says, "Because of the hope of Israel I wear this chain" (28:20). This statement shows the narrator's talent for presenting a vivid picture in words. It is meant to be a memorable picture that conveys the narrator's message: Paul's mission and imprisonment are acts of loyalty to Israel. In the first subscene Paul's statement begins with his claim that he has done nothing opposed to Israel or the Law; it ends with his claim that he is a prisoner for the hope of Israel, thus emphasizing these two related claims of loyalty.

Acts 21:17—26:32, which contains the "final cycle" of speeches in Acts,[15] is carefully constructed as a continuous narrative that builds up to Paul's climactic speech before King Agrippa. The speeches in this section are a series of related, interlacing statements about the issues between Paul and his accusers. Defense against accusations that might concern the Roman authorities plays a relatively minor role, for the primary focus is on the issues between Paul and his fellow Jews.

The hope of Israel is a central theme in this cycle of speeches.[16] I will confine my remarks about the imprisonment speeches to this theme, which is introduced in 23:6 as Paul speaks before the Sanhedrin. There Paul claims that the issue of his trial is "hope and resurrection of the dead." This is strange, for no accusations on these matters have been leveled against Paul. As Paul introduces this subject, he identifies himself as a Pharisee, and his reference to resurrection immediately produces a dispute between the Pharisees and the Sadducees in the Sanhedrin. At this point the reference to hope and resurrection looks very much like a clever ploy to disrupt the proceedings, especially when we note that Paul's statement seems to ignore the real theological issue between himself and his Jewish accusers, namely, his claim that Jesus is the Messiah. However, if we follow this theme of hope and resurrection into the other speeches, we will see its significance grow.

In part it grows through ignoring the initial indication that resurrection is expected by only one branch of Judaism. In 24:15 (cf. 24:21) Paul claims that his hope of resurrection is a hope which "these men themselves await," even though the high priest Ananias, presumably a Sadducee, was among the accusers present. In 26:6-7 it is described as hope in "the promise to our fathers" and the hope of "our twelve tribes" (to dōdekaphylon hēmōn). In 28:20 it is simply called the hope of Israel. Resurrection is not finally a special doctrine of Pharisees or an optional element in Judaism but represents the fulfillment of a promise that is central to Jewish existence, as understood by the narrator.

The impression that Paul is harping on a minor and irrelevant theme also begins to wane when we realize that his reference to the hope of the resurrection has a hidden Christological core. There is a hint of this Christological core in 25:19, but it becomes explicit at the end of Paul's major address before King Agrippa, when Paul speaks of the Messiah who, as "first of the resurrection of the dead, is about to proclaim light both to the people and to the Gentiles"

(26:23). It is the resurrection of Messiah Jesus that fulfills the Jewish hope for the resurrection of the dead. His resurrection initiates a resurrection that others will share.

In the Antioch synagogue Paul previously proclaimed that Jesus' resurrection fulfilled the promise to Israel of a Davidic Messiah. The hope of resurrection is such a weighty matter in Acts because it is also the hope of the messianic kingdom. The "hope of the promise" of resurrection in 26:6-8 is a variation on the "promise" to David of a successor to his throne, which was fulfilled through Jesus' resurrection, according to 13:22-23, 32-37. This connection is supported by a peculiarity of shared language between 13:32 and 26:6. In the one case the promise is *tēn pros tous pateras epangelian genomenēn;* the other verse refers to hope *tēs eis tous pateras hēmōn epangelias genomenēs.* The only use of *epangelia* between these two passages is a reference to the Roman tribune's promise in 23:21. The last major speech of Paul is echoing a theme of his first major speech. According to 26:23 it is "the Messiah" who, through being "first of the resurrection of the dead," proclaims light to the people and the Gentiles. These connections make sense because resurrection life is one of the benefits of sharing in the Messiah's eternal kingdom.[17] This insight explains how Paul can describe resurrection as "the promise to our fathers" for which "our twelve tribes" hope (26:6-8). This is not an individualistic hope for life after death but a hope for the messianic kingdom, which is established through resurrection and characterized by resurrection life.

Paul's emphasis on the hope of Israel is designed to show the continuity between his Pharisaism and his present role as witness of Jesus Messiah. However, this does not explain Paul's reticence (until 26:23) to state that he now believes this hope for resurrection to be fulfilled in Jesus. Jesus is a divisive issue. Paul begins by emphasizing what he has in common with his many Jewish critics. As a good missionary he seeks a point of contact with his audience and from that point of contact attempts to lead them to understand the importance of Jesus. This strategy is indicated by the way that the defense speech before King Agrippa gradually turns into a mission speech. By the end of the speech Paul is no longer talking about his call and his past faithfulness to that call. His past witness to Jesus merges into a present witness: "Until this day I stand bearing witness both to small and to great" (26:22). The missionary significance of the speech is underlined by the concluding dialog with Agrippa, in which Paul appeals to Agrippa's belief in the prophets and Agrippa recognizes that Paul is trying to make him a Christian (26:27-28). Paul is appealing to others as well (26:29). His message is especially designed to appeal to Jews, for it is addressed to those who believe in the prophets, and it concerns the hope of Israel.

These observations raise questions about the view, sometimes asserted on the basis of the end of Acts, that the mission to Jews is a thing of the past for the author of Acts. In his farewell speech to the Ephesian elders (20:18-35), Paul is presented as a model for church leaders, in his dedicated witness to Jews and Greeks (20:21) as well as in other ways. If this is so, it is highly likely that the picture of Paul in the imprisonment narrative, where he is presented as a bold and resourceful missionary who continues his appeal to Jews even in difficult circumstances, is part of the model which the later church should follow.

Nevertheless, the theme of Israel's hope also helps to reveal the tragic irony of Israel's situation. In 26:7 Paul first emphasizes the Jews' intense hope in the promise and then says that he is now being accused by Jews concerning this same hope. The very hope so eagerly sought is rejected when it appears. This is ironic; it is also tragic, for Israel is losing what rightly belongs to it. The same tragic irony is conveyed in 28:20 by the image of Paul in chains for the hope of Israel. The messenger who proclaims the fulfillment of Israel's hope should be honored by Israel. Instead, Paul wears a chain because of his faithfulness to Israel's hope. This means suffering for Paul. It is an even greater tragedy for Israel.[18] This sense of tragic irony carries over into the second subscene (28:23-28) of Paul's encounter with the Jews of Rome and is forcefully expressed through the quotation from Isaiah.

This second subscene reminds us of previous occasions when Paul responded to Jewish resistance by announcing that he was turning to the Gentiles. However, there are some differences. Paul is not preaching in a synagogue. This change, to be sure, simply reflects Paul's imprisonment. It is still clear that Paul is addressing a Jewish assembly. The difference in the description of the Jews' reaction may be more significant. Instead of a report that Paul turns to the Gentiles when there is public reviling or blaspheming, we are simply told that the Jews disagreed among themselves, some being persuaded and some disbelieving (28:24). Paul's reaction makes clear that his intensive efforts ("from early morning until evening") have not been successful, so it is unlikely that the reference to some "being persuaded" *(epeithonto)* means that they have committed themselves to the Christian way. Probably the use of the imperfect is significant: they were in process of being persuaded but had made no lasting decision.[19] Why would the narrator want to say this when the scene is building up to the bitter words of Isaiah? Use of the quotation would seem most justified if the rejection is total. Furthermore, if the scene's purpose is to show that there is no longer any hope of convincing Jews and that the church must now concentrate exclusively on the Gentile mission, the point is undermined by portraying part of the Jewish assembly on the verge of acceptance. The reference to some being persuaded indicates that there is still hope of convincing some Jews in spite of what Paul is about to say about the Jewish community. While the Jewish community (controlled by its leadership) is deaf and blind, there are still those within it who are open to the Christian message. To indicate this, the narrator chose not to make the Jewish reaction as completely negative as we might expect.

The harsh words of the quotation are nevertheless appropriate. Paul's preaching on this day was a special opportunity to speak to the Jewish community of Rome, which is now departing without accepting Paul's witness. The presence of disagreement among the Jews is enough to show that Paul has not achieved what he sought. He was seeking a communal decision, a recognition by the Jewish community as a whole that Jesus is the fulfillment of the Jewish hope. The presence of significant opposition shows that this is not going to happen. Previous scenes have shown that the opposition of some can make preaching to the Jewish assembly impossible. Paul's closing statement in 28:25-28 is a response to this hard fact.

In spite of their failure to accept his witness, Paul still has a message for the Roman Jews. He must take the role of the prophet Isaiah and respeak his words,[20] words so bitter for both prophet and people that Isaiah cried out, "How long?" (Isa. 6:11). Isaiah's words are full of ironic tension that expresses the tension in the plot of Acts at its end. Through repeated and emphatic statements, the people are told of a highly unnatural situation: ears, eyes, and heart, which are meant for hearing, seeing, and understanding, have lost their power to perceive. This unnatural state, in which the organs of perception contradict their own purpose, has blocked God's desire to "heal them," a desire that a perceptive people would gladly embrace. But God has not finished speaking to this people, for it is the prophet's uncomfortable task to show unbelieving Israel its self-contradiction. He is told to "go to this people and say"[21] the bitter and anguished words that disclose Israel's failure. Both prophet and people are caught in this situation of tragic irony, for the prophet is commanded to speak to a people that cannot understand. Paul assumes this prophetic task. He again speaks to Israel, trying to make the people see their blindness and hear their deafness.[22]

Acts ends on a tragic, not a triumphant note. This is not lessened by 28:28. The function of these concluding words about the Gentiles is not to justify the Gentile mission, which has been done long ago, but to jar the Roman Jews by the contrast between their deafness and the Gentiles' readiness to hear. This is a message to the Roman Jews ("Let it be known to you . . ."). It says, "They will hear," but you will not. This ironic reversal is strengthened by noting that Paul's announcement is a striking shift from his earlier announcement in the Antioch synagogue. There he proclaimed, "To us the word of this salvation has been sent out *(exapestalē)*" (13:26). But to Jews who are deaf and blind he says, "To the Gentiles has been sent *(apestalē)* this salvation of God; *they* will hear."

Paul is speaking to the Jews of Rome, not to Jews everywhere. Yet the theme of Jewish rejection, followed by mission to the Gentiles, is highlighted in major scenes at the beginning and end of Paul's mission and is repeated in other scenes. These connected scenes suggest a pattern or trend, even though there are exceptions. Building a pattern through individual scenes allows the narrator to avoid the implication that Jewish response was always the same, while suggesting the direction in which events are moving.

In previous scenes the announcement of turning to the Gentiles did not exclude renewed Jewish mission in other cities. Nothing prevents us from understanding the announcement in 28:28 as applying to Rome, leaving open the possibility of preaching to Jews elsewhere. Yet such an announcement at the end of a narrative carries extra weight. Just because the narrative ends, the narrator grants the final situation a certain permanence. The narrator may have been willing to do this because of awareness that the possibility of Christians preaching to a Jewish assembly, such as Paul addressed in Rome, has become very remote. Nevertheless, there are signs of the narrator's concern to keep a mission to Jews alive in spite of this situation. Even after Paul is forced to abandon his preaching in the synagogues of Corinth and Ephesus, the narrator indicates that the mission reaches Jews of those cities (18:8; 19:10, 17-18).[23] In Ephesus, especially, there is indication of a preaching mission to Jews after Paul leaves the synagogue. There Paul preached for two years, with the result that "all those inhabiting Asia heard the word of the Lord, both Jews and Greeks" (19:10). This remark is placed after Paul's withdrawal from the synagogue. The Jews mentioned cannot be limited to those encountered in the synagogue of Ephesus before Paul's departure. Even if we allow for exaggeration, we must recognize that Paul's continuing preaching brings him in contact with a much wider circle of Jews than those who attended the synagogue of Ephesus.[24] Paul's continuing mission to both Jews and Gentiles in Ephesus provides a precedent for understanding his continuing mission in Rome, described in 28:30-31.

We have already noted that there are individuals within the Jewish community in Rome who show openness toward the Christian message (28:24). We have also noted that the lengthy imprisonment narrative presents Paul as a Jew who continues to witness to Jews in spite of their vigorous attempts to do away with him, and I have suggested that in this as in other respects Paul is a model for later evangelists. The summary of Paul's continuing preaching in 28:30-31 provides some additional evidence. After the preceding contrast between Jews and Gentiles, the reference in 28:30 to Paul welcoming "all" those coming to him should not be dismissed as an idle remark. According to 28:24, some of the Jews Paul had addressed were being persuaded by his message. This provides a motivation for some of them coming to talk to him later. Acts 28:30 makes clear that any Jews or Gentiles who did come were welcomed by Paul, who continued to preach to them and teach. Note that Paul's preaching and teaching focuses on "the reign of God" and "the things concerning the Lord Jesus Messiah." These are the themes of Paul's preaching to the Roman Jews in 28:23. The distinctive speeches in Lystra (14:15-17) and Athens (17:22-31) show awareness that the mission cannot begin with pure Gentiles in the same way as Jews. Yet Paul in Rome continues to preach the themes with which he had addressed the Jews, suggesting that Jews are at least included in his audience.

The special connection of "the reign of God" and "the Lord Jesus Messiah" with a Jewish setting is indicated by some other observations. While Acts twice refers to God's reign in statements to established Christian communities (14:22; 20:25), which could include Gentiles (and in which Gentile members could have been instructed in such Jewish matters), the term is used elsewhere in addressing Jews or Samaritans (1:3,6; 8:12; 19:8; 28:23). This is especially appropriate because the theme of God's reign is connected in Luke-Acts with Jesus' own reign as the Davidic Messiah. Lukan interest in Jesus' kingship appears in Luke 19:38 (which differs from Matthew and Mark); 22:29-30; 23:42, and in the passages which present Jesus as the successor to David's throne (Luke 1:32-33,69-70; Acts 2:25-36; 13:22-23,32-37). The centrality of Jesus' kingship in God's reign explains the repeated dual description of the preacher's message in Acts 8:12; 28:23,31. It concerns both God's reign and Jesus. The missionaries are not preaching about two separate things. They are preaching about the realization of God's reign through the enthronement of Jesus at God's right hand as royal Messiah. It is sometimes noted that the reference to "the reign of God" in 28:31 forms an inclusion with the similar reference in 1:3.[25] The reference in 28:31 to the "Lord Jesus Messiah" also forms an inclusion with the climax of the Pentecost speech in 2:36. "The Lord Jesus Messiah" briefly summarizes Peter's proclamation of Jesus as "both Lord and Messiah," Messiah because he fulfills God's oath to David, and Lord because he is seated at God's right hand, a proclamation that Paul repeated (with variations) in his synagogue sermon in Acts 13. At the end of Acts, Paul is presented as faithfully continuing the message which he and Peter preached to the Jews in the major sermons near the beginning of the narratives about their ministries.[26] The situation has changed in that Paul can no longer speak in synagogues or to the Jews assembled as a community. But he continues to welcome all people who are willing to hear his message, including Jews.

The indication in 28:24 that some Jews are receptive and the description of Paul's activity in 28:30-31 both suggest that Paul's audience continues to include Jews, and this view is supported by the precedent of Paul's preaching in Ephesus after leaving the synagogue (19:10). Furthermore, this interpretation fits the portrait of Paul's mission as a whole. To the very end Paul remains faithful to the Lord's calling to bear witness to both Jews and Gentiles (9:15; 22:15; 26:16-18 [cf. 26:23]). Neither Jewish rejection nor Roman imprisonment prevent him from preaching "with all boldness" in response to this call. The final verses of Acts picture Paul doing what he told the Ephesian elders he must do: complete his ministry from the Lord in spite of the threat of death, a ministry of witnessing to both Jews and Greeks (cf. 20:21,24). This is the image of Paul with which the narrator chooses to leave us.

Discussion of the Lukan attitude toward Israel must take account of two fundamental points: a persistent concern with the realization of scriptural promises which, the narrator recognizes, apply first of all to the Jewish people, and the stinging experience of rejection of the message that the hope of Israel is now being fulfilled. The resulting tension, especially apparent in the tension between the promise in the Antioch sermon and the bitter words at the end of Acts, is not resolved in the narrative. Acts offers no solution except the patient and persistent preaching of the gospel in hope that the situation will change.

The situation has not changed. Therefore, the assumption that the promises to the Jews will be realized primarily through their acceptance of the Christian message is now doubtful not only to Jews but also to many Christians. The passionate concern in Luke-Acts that God's salvation be realized comprehensively—for both Jews and Gentiles—is still important, but, in my opinion, it is now necessary to recognize the diverse ways in which different groups will find that salvation and express its meaning for their lives.

7

THE MISSION TO THE JEWS IN ACTS: UNRAVELING LUKE'S "MYTH OF THE 'MYRIADS'"

Michael J. Cook

Adiscussion I once had with the late Samuel Sandmel envisioned an editorial—the one appearing in Antioch of Pisidia's Jewish tabloid the day after Paul visited their synagogue:

Itinerants claiming to be Jews arrive in our city, are treated hospitably and welcomed in our synagogue, and are allowed to preach to us. In their preaching they say things that some of us find either incredible or distasteful or both. Why, if they know our beliefs, have they bothered to come to our synagogue? Why did they cause an uproar? Why did they not hire their own hall and leave us Jews alone? Why do they claim to be Jews when in their life-style and in what they advocate they express views about the Law . . . that go against what we have always espoused? We would not have had uproars in our synagogue if these people had not intruded. It was only when they violated our hospitality that some of our people were moved to throw them out as unwelcome troublemakers.[1]

This imagined account of happenings in Pisidian Antioch complements Luke's own version, in Acts 13:14-51—though Luke, of course, presents the visitors' perspective, not the hosts'. Such a reaction by Jewish hosts, we might surmise, could have held equally true for other Jewish communities as well. Luke himself suggests as much.[2]

Yet some scholars would insist that, aside from his narrating particular instances of rejection, there are times when Luke seems optimistic concerning the possibility of Christian successes with Jews. Such an impression appears unmistakable in view of Luke's insistence that, initially, "myriads"[3] of Jews not only listened to Christian preachers but also joined the new movement! Paul's own epistles bring Luke's portrait into higher relief, for Paul assesses the mission to the Jews as having been, for the most part, unsuccessful.[4] This personal appraisal renders all the more puzzling Luke's claim that Jews had originally flocked to Christianity's ranks!

Such contradictory impressions occasion questions. Does a special Lukan motive underlie his unusual presentation? Are we to infer, as some have argued, that Luke was still interested in reaching the Jews of his own day and that he was in some sense sympathetically disposed toward all or some of them—hence his positive assessment of the successes of early missions in gaining Jewish believers? And what bearing might this have in explaining the curious behavior of the Lukan Paul, who resumes his mission to the Jews not only in the face of recurrent failures, but despite his repeated protests that "from now on" he is through with them forever? Is there a basis, moreover, for concluding with some that Luke himself was a Gentile adherent of Judaism or, indeed, a Jewish Christian[5]—and that this might somehow explain his characteristic position? These are among the considerations with which to wrestle in responding to Robert C. Tannehill's stimulating essay.[6]

I have long and consistently admired the meticulous care and persuasive argumentation which characterize Tannehill's writings. In his present essay, repeated demonstrations of how passages in diverse segments of Luke-Acts resonate against one another reflect not merely the skill of the Lukan narrator but also Tannehill's own extraordinary insight. I am thus hardly surprised to discover myself in virtually total agreement with much of his analysis. At the same time, I am disconcerted by two problems surfacing only near the end of his essay, both related, in some degree, to the complex of puzzles just listed. I cannot agree with Tannehill's suggestions (1) that the narrator of Acts is advocating the church's continued mission to the Jews in his own day and (2) that Luke portrays the rejection of the Jews as tragic, or as a situation of tragic irony.[7]

Accordingly, my response will be more useful if I devote my remarks, in the main, to addressing these two areas of disagreement.

I. SOME PROBLEMATIC ASPECTS OF TANNEHILL'S INTERPRETATION

Is Luke, through the book of Acts, urging a continued mission to the Jews in his own day? This suggestion surfaces at least four times in the latter part of Tannehill's essay. He notes how Paul continues his appeal to the Jews even during the difficult circumstances of the imprisonment narrative and concludes that Luke intends Paul's persistent overtures to the Jews to serve as a model which the later church should emulate. The pattern of the past (as in Corinth and Ephesus) has indeed been to indicate at least some success in Paul's missions to Jews even after Paul is forced to abandon preaching in their synagogues. By repeatedly highlighting the presence of disagreement among the Jews whom Paul addresses, by repeatedly portraying some Jews as at least listening to Paul, Luke is allegedly signaling the church in the late first century likewise to maintain the mission to the Jews as an ongoing concern.

I do appreciate the ambiguities in the text which open the way for Tannehill's interpretation. At the same time, the problem of Luke's audience demands attention. Would they have readily picked up on this alleged Lukan intent?[8] Many New Testament scholars pore over these texts without sensing any Lukan advocacy of a continued mission to the Jews of his own day. Would average Lukan reader/hearers[9] of the late first (indeed, any) century have gotten the same impression as that inferred by Tannehill? No—indeed, exactly the opposite impression would probably have been forthcoming, stimulated particularly by those glaring passages, abrasive toward Jews, which reader/hearers would be least likely to overlook or interpret in other than a straightforward fashion. These include:

Since you thrust [the word of God] from you, and judge yourselves unworthy of eternal life, behold, we turn to the *Gentiles*.[10] (Acts 13:46)

Paul was occupied with preaching, testifying to the Jews that the Christ was Jesus. And when they opposed and reviled him, he shook out his garments and said to them, "Your blood be upon your heads! I am innocent. *From now on* I will go to the *Gentiles*." (Acts 18:5b-6)

Paul . . . made one statement: "The Holy Spirit was right in saying to your fathers through Isaiah the prophet: '. . . You shall indeed hear but *never* understand, and you shall indeed see but *never* perceive. . . .' Let it be known to you then that this salvation of God has been sent to the *Gentiles; they* will listen." (Acts 28:25-28)

Most might infer from these passages not simply that the mission to the Jews was over in Luke's day but also that it had already been terminated by Paul himself even decades earlier!

If Luke actually intended to say what Tannehill believes, then why, given his stated desire in his own prolog "to write an orderly account" clearly conveying the truth (Luke 1:3-4), did not Luke just say what he wanted to say—forthrightly and *un*ambiguously? In Romans, Paul says what *he* means about the prospects of bringing Jews into the fold—no camouflaged intimations! There, the genuine (as opposed to the Lukan) Paul, while admitting his own lack of significant success among Jews, nonetheless speaks clearly of Israel's eventual "full inclusion" and "acceptance," explaining that the "hardening [which] has come upon part of Israel [is only] until the full number of the Gentiles come in . . . [when] all Israel will be saved" (Rom. 11:12,15,25-26). If Luke wanted the mission to Jews continued, as Tannehill thinks, could he not at least have had *his* version of Paul clearly convey: "In spite of their opaqueness, keep the mission to the Jews going"? Why cannot the Lukan Paul be as clear on this one issue as is the genuine Paul (who, on most issues, is hardly known for clarity)?

If indeed Luke's audience would not have interpreted Acts the way Tannehill does, how decisive should this consideration be? For some, the matter of audience comprehension is debatable. No justice to the richness of Luke-Acts will be done by becoming excessively absorbed with what Luke's audience would or would not intuit. When scholars render the hidden or subtle more explicit, they may also, thereby, render a well-deserved service to an author. In the present case, however, we are faced with a quandary: what Tannehill gathers from Luke seems to run not only deeper than, but counter to, the natural inference by Luke's audience! The possibility surfaces, therefore, that Tannehill's interpretation also runs counter to what Luke intended.

To be sure, the *inferred* meaning of an ancient work may be different for audiences of a later day, such as our own—and, in some schools of thought, it has become entirely valid to assess the message and relevance of a work on such a changed basis. Yet Tannehill's study is ostensibly devoted to exploring Luke's actual intent per se, i.e., what *Luke* means, over and above whatever meaning *we* might discover in Luke. I would submit, accordingly, that, unless we dispute Luke's ability to communicate with clarity, we simply have to pay due regard to what Luke's audience—those for whom he wrote in his own day—might naturally have inferred him to mean. Most would probably have called to mind those jarring denunciations of the Jews already cited (Acts 13:46; 18:6; and 28:28), echoed especially by the ringing indictment, drawn from Isaiah, that the Jews will "*never* understand . . . and *never* perceive." Luke's very allowance of the word "never" only six verses from the end of Acts is curiously discouraging in a work alleged to be advocating a renewal of mission! The most plausible reason for Luke's readers to miss the (Tannehill) point is, starkly stated, that this was simply not Luke's point! Rather, by the end of Luke-Acts, for Luke as well as for his audience, the earlier thousands of believing Jews are now long-forgotten, and the volumes' final words are "a distillation of the author's controlling concept . . . [that] the failed mission to the Jews is terminated in favor of the mission to the Gentiles."[11]

Nonetheless, those diverging from Tannehill must advance an alternative resolution of the problems to which he rightly summons our attention: if Luke is not urging a continued mission to the Jews, then why does he repeatedly attest that missionizing among Jews had originally been successful? Why does Luke repeatedly portray Jewish audiences as having been divided among themselves over Paul's message? And why does Luke have Paul repeatedly resume his mission to Jews of another, new community when each time, on the heels of failure, he has sworn them off, insisting that henceforth he will go only to Gentiles?

Literary Patterns?

Might part of the solution lie with literary patterns? For example, while studying the genre of sea voyages in ancient Mediterranean literature—in conjunction with his analysis of the "we-passages" in Acts—Vernon K. Robbins[12] discovered a pattern reminiscent of various of Paul's experiences in Acts: when visitors arrive in a community, initially the natives are friendly toward the travelers. Then an event occurs which divides the natives over whether or not the visitors are to be trusted. The spokesman for the visitors is now put to the test, particularly his abilities to speak persuasively. Joseph B. Tyson,[13] meanwhile, in a study confined to Luke-Acts, analyzed another literary pattern: a crowd's *sudden reaction-reversal*. Thus, while crowds initially approve of Paul, they abruptly and startlingly reverse themselves. The literary effect of this unexpected disappearance of popular support is to spotlight Paul himself, standing now alone, just as Jesus did in his trials.[14]

To some, these treatments might suggest application to the same problems in Acts which Tannehill addresses—yet with a significantly different conclusion. In the former study,[15] the presence of initial positive audience reaction is identified as only an aspect of a literary pattern. If this were likewise the case with a number of Paul's episodes in Acts, then the motifs of Jews initially accepting Christianity, or of Jewish audiences being divided over what they hear, could be accounted for merely in this fashion (ascribed to the operation of a literary pattern)—without any attendant inference that Luke was thereby endorsing a continued mission to Jews of his own day.

On the basis of Tyson's study, meanwhile, the initial thousands of Jewish converts in Acts would seem to serve a different function from that in the pattern discovered by Robbins. With respect to Tannehill's position, however, essentially the same conclusion would ultimately apply: if Luke enlists a positive Jewish audience disposition only as a preliminary to the crowd's sudden reaction-reversal, then once again it is unwarranted to detect in these passages any Lukan advocacy of a continued mission to the Jews—particularly since "traces of the pattern . . . may be found [even] in some narratives that deal with *Gentiles*"![16]

Tyson's theory would resolve an anomaly central to Tannehill's essay: a pattern of initially-positive-response and subsequent-abrupt-reversal, when replicated in a succession of distinct communities (Pisidian Antioch [Acts 13:13-52], Iconium [14:1-2], Thessalonica [17:1-9], Beroea [17:10-15], Ephesus [19:8-10]), would inevitably conjure up the same peculiar picture we have of Paul in Acts— where, despite suffering repeated rejections, he readily resumes overtures to Jews even in instances when he has but recently vowed to sever his ties with them! Tyson's intent seems evident: in order for the pattern of initial-acceptance/reaction-reversal to be replicated in cases involving the-Jewish-public-in-relation-to-Paul, Paul must be *made* to embark on renewed missions to the Jews despite recent rejections. Otherwise, how would a new public have the opportunity to welcome him as a prelude to turning abruptly against him? Accordingly, when "the Lukan Paul rejects a continuing mission to Jews [only shortly thereafter to resume it] . . . he must resume it because the *literary pattern* demands it." [17] If it is a literary pattern which actually governs Paul's behavior, then we would do well to reconsider—also to relinquish—the notion that Luke is here, through the figure of Paul, expressing his advocacy of a continued mission to the Jews.

The effect of Tyson's study, when applied to the problem at hand, is to divert attention from the apparent inconsistent behavior on the part of the Lukan Paul to that, instead, on the part of the Jewish public. To Luke's audience, the latter inconsistency would seem equally if not more conspicuous—illustrated in many instances, yet nowhere more dramatically than on the grandest scale: the contrast between the closing chapters of the Gospel and the opening chapters of Acts! Reading both works consecutively, we discover "that the *same* public that [has just] bitterly rejected Jesus [has now] enthusiastically accepted the early Christians . . . [an] apparent inconsistency. . . created by the use of the same literary pattern in the two volumes." [18]

It is crucial to recognize that the Lukan Paul, in his behavior, is often only reactive to how the Jewish public behaves toward him! Thus, while his unexpected resumptions of missions to Jews are, in large measure, occasioned by the literary pattern impinging upon him, the prime mover of that pattern is, nonetheless, the Jewish public, not Paul! This warranted shift of our focus from Paul to the Jewish public carries with it an important ramification: it may be ill-advised to preoccupy ourselves, as Tannehill apparently does, with how the Lukan Paul resumes missions to the Jews. Since these actions are largely but a by-product of the Jewish public's behavior— governed, in turn, by a literary pattern—the motif of Paul's renewed overtures may, in a sense, be somewhat secondary even as far as Luke himself is concerned!

But if this is true with Paul's actions, it is hardly the case with Paul's words. Here, in fact, is an instance when "words speak louder than actions!'' Paul's resumptions of missions to the Jews are not as important in and of themselves as what Paul says to the Jews when they reverse their acceptance and then reject him! For Paul's words are not predetermined by the literary pattern in the same way his actions are. This is why his glaring, abrasive denunciations of the Jews (Acts 13:46; 18:6; 28:25-28) are indeed a medium through which Luke's actual intent may be gauged—a conclusion that would complement not only that of those many scholars who interpret Luke as condemnatory of the Jews, but also that naturally drawn by Luke's lay audience. This is why I find Tannehill's interpretation problematic: it pursues, after all, what I feel is a wrong clue, determining Luke's intent from the Lukan Paul's actions rather than his words!

My applications of these studies by Robbins and particularly by Tyson have suggested that passages Tannehill construes one way lend themselves, at the very least, to alternative interpretations as well—and if not these alternatives, then possibly some other. In fact, such an other alternative is, I believe, very much required if only because recourse to literary patterns alone leaves a significant dilemma unresolved: if Luke has relinquished all interest in, as well as hope for, the viability of a continuing mission to the Jews, then what purpose is served by his insistence that "myriads" of Jews had initially gravitated to the Christian preachment? This very insistence is what has provoked the most confusion! I agree that a literary pattern is operative and that this readily accounts (1) for Jewish audiences, in toto or in part, responding favorably to a Christian preacher—as a prerequisite for their inevitable reaction-reversal and (2) for the Lukan Paul's repeated resumptions of his mission to Jews. But why does Luke incorporate this pattern in the first place? In the service of what overarching objective has it been enlisted by him? In addressing this concern, we would do well to give added attention to another Lukan emphasis.

Luke's Understanding of Christianity as Embodying Authentic Judaism

One of the predominant Lukan interests is to cast Christianity as the direct perpetuation of authentic Judaism. The Lukan texts at issue, which have been isolated by Tannehill, may be profitably pursued as reflections of this one Lukan priority! Much of my response to

Tannehill will be predicated on this fundamental observation. Accordingly, it is necessary to document my view in some detail, through an excursus of sorts, in order to demonstrate its applicability to the subject at hand.

While many scholars prefer to speak of the theme "*Whom* does Luke consider the true Israel?" it is more productive to ask, "*What* does Luke feel embodies the authentic Judaism?" When scholars focus on the Who? rather than the What? Luke-Acts emerges as recalcitrant and confusing—and there ensue explanations of Luke's intent often reflecting, in my opinion, more the ingenuity of the exegete than anything intended by Luke or naturally inferable by Luke's average audience. It then becomes arduous to reconcile the diverse statements Luke does make about the Jews: his recurrent indictments of them, on the one hand, and attestations of their "myriad" conversions, on the other. Since the resulting inconsistencies seem to defy resolution, I have found the struggles of others to explain them unconvincing.

When, however, we shift our focus from the Who? to the What? such difficulties recede significantly, confirming that now we are indeed addressing a question Luke himself is genuinely posing: What embodies authentic Judaism? His answer: Christianity! With this as our central question, we will later be in a position to discuss both who the Jews are and who they are not in Luke-Acts.

Literally dozens of illustrations spring to mind demonstrating that, in Luke-Acts, Christianity has been brought into meticulous correspondence with what is symbolically central in Judaism. This concern governs, to begin with, Luke's repeated conformance of Jesus' religious life to models of Jewish custom—by means of details unmentioned (or unemphasized) in other Gospels: specifications of Jesus' circumcision on the eighth day, and his conveyance to the Temple for a *pidyon-haben* (redemption of the firstborn) ceremony;[19] of his family's recurrent Passover pilgrimages to Jerusalem, not to mention his personal presence in the temple at age 12, instructing none other than the very sages of Judaism (Luke 2:41ff.); later on, of his customary attendance together with his teaching "in their synagogues,"[20] and of his daily preaching in the temple (Luke 19:47; 20:1; 21:37-38). Those loyal to Jesus are similarly portrayed: thus, the women, who intend to come to the tomb, first rest on the Sabbath "according to the commandment" (Luke 23:56). Following the resurrection appearances, those "who believed" are continually in the temple itself (Acts 2:46; 3:1; 5:42), "blessing God" (Luke 24:53). Luke frequently implies that the fidelity of Jesus and his followers to Judaism sharply contrasts with the infidelity of Jews themselves! The new movement remains fully continuous with the parent, as opposed to Jews who have gone astray![21]

In the case of Paul, this same motif accounts for many divergencies by Acts from Paul's genuine Epistles. This is why only Acts tells us of Paul's upbringing at the feet of the great Pharisaic sage, Gamaliel I (Acts 22:3), a touch which, however implausible,[22] renders Paul representative of the very center of Palestinian Judaism—or so, at least, it might have been construed during the Jamnia period, Luke's own day, when the rabbinic leader, another Gamaliel (II), may have been widely known even in the Diaspora. Only Acts furnishes Paul with a Hebrew name (Acts 13:9), as well as facility in the Hebrew language (21:40—22:2)—though the "Bible" of Paul's Epistles is hardly the "Bible" in Hebrew. Only Acts relates Paul's circumcision of Timothy[23] (in contrast, in the Epistles, to his position vis-à-vis Titus, Gal. 2:3), here again intimating the Jewish fidelity of important Christians. A similar pattern is seen in the Lukan Paul's willingness (however incomprehensible on the basis of the Epistles) to cut his hair in fulfilling a legal vow,[24] in his haste to by-pass Ephesus so as to reach Jerusalem by Pentecost (Acts 20:16), and, naturally, in his regular presence in the temple (e.g., Acts 22:17; cf. 24:11; 26:21).

The pattern becomes especially disconcerting when the Lukan Paul accedes to James' request—he actually cooperates in allaying false(?) suspicions that he has undermined Jewish Law![25] More problematic than Paul's consenting to the Law (purifying himself with four men under a vow and paying their expenses) is the apparent hypocrisy Luke is comfortable imputing to him.[26]

Particularly troubling, also, is the manner by which characteristic elements of Pauline theology are casualties of this Lukan process! Luke's formulation that only "with respect to the hope and the resurrection of the dead I [Paul] am on trial" entirely distracts us from Pauline doctrines which indeed did distinguish him from Judaism, e.g., justification by faith, and the annulment of the Law of Moses.[27]

In demonstrating Christianity's firm foundation in Judaism, Luke enlists geography as well. He fixes Jesus' postresurrection appearances not in a region on the fringe of Judaism (Galilee),[28] but rather in the geographic core of Judaism (the environs of Jerusalem);[29] nor does he allow the Twelve to flee to Galilee[30] or even to depart from Jerusalem (Acts 1:4)—because he requires them in Jerusalem so the church can emanate from the center of Judaism.[31] Accordingly, Luke makes necessary adjustments, omitting, for example, anticipations of Jesus' appearances in Galilee, such as we find in Mark and Matthew.[32]

Other Lukan emphases on Jerusalem abound not only in the Gospel[33] but in Acts, particularly in connection with Paul. Thus, Luke insists that Paul, in addition to being "brought up" and "educated" in Jerusalem (Acts 22:3; 26:4), also experienced the risen Christ during a trip commencing from (and commissioned by authorities of) Jerusalem (Acts 9:1-3; 22:5; 26:10,12). Both motifs, the journey and the commission, are patently artificial. The historicity of the Jerusalem/road-to-Damascus trip (even disregarding its three differing formulations, Acts 9:3-9; 22:6-11; 26:12-18) is as suspect as other Lukan travel-motifs: Mary's visit to Elizabeth (Luke 1:39-56); the Bethlehem sojourn of Joseph and Mary;[34] Jesus' "stay[ing] . . . behind" after a Passover pilgrimage to Jerusalem with his family;[35] his extended excursion through Samaria (Luke 9:51ff.); Herod Antipas's coincidental presence in Jerusalem (23:7ff.);[36] even the cancellation of the apostles' flight to Galilee. These examples raise questions, of course, about the reliability of travel episodes in Acts as well![37]

Moreover, while Paul had indeed persecuted the church in the Diaspora,[38] what evidence demonstrates that it would have been necessary to secure a Jerusalem commission to do so? Did Jerusalem priests have such extra-Judean authority? That Paul personally visited the high priest, expressly to solicit extradition letters, is as doubtful[39] as his early presence in Jerusalem to start with! As Paul himself insists in his genuine writings, even some years after experiencing a revelation of the Christ, he still remained "not known by sight to the churches of Christ in Judea" (Gal. 1:15-23). This declaration contrasts sharply with statements, forthcoming from Acts, suggesting that he had achieved an infamous reputation among Christians early on in Jerusalem itself (Acts 22:19-20; 26:10-11a). The chronological accounting in Acts is also suspect: the three-year lapse before Paul went up to Jerusalem (in Galatians) seems telescoped by Luke (Gal 1:18; Acts 9:19,23,26; cf. 26:19-20). There is sufficient reason to doubt whether any of these "Jerusalem connections" in Luke is more plausible than Paul's Jerusalem connection with Gamaliel.

The above complex of multiple intertwining motifs is hardly comprehensible on the basis of the Epistles alone (actually, not on the basis of the Epistles at all!). Yet the interaction of these motifs is readily explicable on the view that Luke is preoccupied with demonstrating Christianity's foundation in, and extension/augmentation of, the central core of Judaism.

This same concern is manifested as much by Luke's attenuations as by his accentuations. Thus, Luke de-emphasizes numerous impressions of opposition, on the part of either Jesus or Paul, to Jewish institutions, and vice versa; for undue emphasis on traditions of conflict, or even contrast, would tend to call into question the consonance he wishes to establish for Christianity vis-à-vis Judaism. I am hardly arguing that Luke eliminates such impressions altogether—only that he de-emphasizes, weakens them. Elimination would be manifestly impossible, for though he advances Christianity as extending authentic Judaism, Luke is nonetheless opposed to the Jews themselves, and only a fine line distinguished Jewish institutions from the Jews! Nonetheless, certain attenuations are quite evident. Consider, for example, how he dilutes (not eliminates) the cleansing of the temple episode, and note both what Luke omits from Mark and also adds and revises:

Matt. 21:12-13	*Mark 11:15-27*	*Luke 19:45-20:1*
And Jesus entered the temple of God and drove out all who sold and bought in the temple, *and he overturned the tables of the money-changers and the seats of those who sold pigeons.* . . .	And he entered the temple and began to drive out those who sold and those who bought in the temple, *and he overturned the tables of the money-changers and the seats of those who sold pigeons.* . . .	And he entered the temple and began to drive out those who sold. . . .
		And he was teaching daily in the temple.
	And the chief priests and the scribes	The chief priests and the scribes and the

113

	heard it and sought a way to destroy him. . . . And they came again to Jerusalem.	principal men of the people sought to destroy him. . . .
And when he entered the temple. . . .	And as he was walking in the temple. . . .	One day, as he was *teaching the people in* the temple. . . .

Since the temple represents the major institution of Judaism, Luke sets about toning down indications by Mark of Jesus' militancy against it, omitting, for example, the recounting of Jesus' overturning of the tables of money-changers and the seats of those who sold pigeons. Note, moreover, how Luke also minimizes the effect of the cleansing! In Mark, the cleansing is an action which provokes a reaction (the decision by the Jewish authorities "to destroy him"). But with Luke, the cleansing becomes an action which elicits no immediate reaction. Of course, the authorities still "sought to destroy him"; but, by omitting the Markan clause that the chief priests and the scribes had "heard it" (i.e., "heard" what Jesus had done in the temple), and adding a clause concerning Jesus' teaching, Luke has severed the connection Mark established between the cleansing and the authorities' consequent plot to do Jesus in. Luke has Jesus continuing in the temple, "teaching daily," as if, so to speak, the cleansing had never occurred! It might even be inferred that Jesus' arrest had been triggered by his "teaching daily in the temple," not by his "cleansing" it!

Similarly, in rendering the charges he says were lodged against Jesus, Luke includes no threat against the temple. This accounts, in part, for his abbreviating the scene in the Sanhedrin: instead of the witnesses' attesting to Jesus' stated intention, as in Mark ("we heard him say, 'I will destroy this temple . . .' "), or to Jesus' affirmation of capability, as in Matthew ("this fellow said, 'I am able to destroy the temple of God . . .' "), in Luke there is no corresponding statement.[40] Elsewhere, as well, the "temple charge" is omitted:

Matt. 27:39-40	*Mark 15:29-30*	*Luke 23:37*
And those who passed by derided him, wagging their heads, and	And those who passed by derided him, wagging their heads, and	and

114

saying, "*You who would destroy the temple and build it in three days,*	saying, "Aha! *You who would destroy the temple and build it in three days,*	saying,
		"If you are the King of the Jews
save yourself! . . ."	save yourself . . .!"	save yourself!"

Analogous to Luke's treatment of the temple is his handling of Jesus in relation to other Jewish institutions: the high priest and Sanhedrin, for example. The consequence is that, unlike the pronouncement of judgment we discover in Mark and Matthew, in Luke Jesus is not formally condemned by high priest or Sanhedrin before he is taken to Pilate:

Matt. 26:65-66	*Mark 14:63-64*	*Luke 22:71*
Then *the high priest* tore his robes, and said, "He has uttered blasphemy. Why do we still need witnesses? You have now heard his *blasphemy.*	And *the high priest* tore his mantle, and said, "Why do we still need witnesses? You have heard his *blasphemy.*	And *they* said, "What further testimony do we need? We have heard *it* ourselves from his own lips."
What is your judgment?" They answered. "He deserves death."	*What is your decision?"* And they all condemned him as deserving death. . . .	

In Luke's Gospel, the high priest's role is significantly diminished,[41] and no "decision" (Mark) or "judgment" (Matthew) is rendered.

Moreover, Luke advances the mocking of Jesus so that it precedes the hearing before the high priest. Unlike Mark and Matthew, therefore, Luke withholds any legal justification from the mocking and beating of Jesus, since the Sanhedrin has yet to convene! While Luke has Jesus maltreated by "the men who were holding" him, this abuse is not formally attributable to any official decision by a Jewish institution.[42]

When Luke does have the Jews advance a bill of particulars against Jesus, the accusations again do not show Jesus to be disloyal to Jewish *institutions:* "And they began to accuse him, saying, 'We found this man perverting our nation, and forbidding us to give tribute to Caesar, and saying that he himself is Christ a king' " (Luke 23:2). Even though each Evangelist portrays charges against Jesus as self-evidently false, in Luke even false bills of particulars, while not eliminated, are nonetheless toned down with respect to their intimations of disloyalty to, or tension with, Jewish institutions, whether the temple, the Sanhedrin, or the high priest (whose slave Jesus even protects! Luke 22:50-51).[43]

As we might expect, this very same dynamic explains the Lukan Paul's relations with Jewish institutions as well! He is instructed by none other than Gamaliel (the first, Acts 22:3), the outstanding Pharisee in the Sanhedrin (who earlier had counseled moderation in dealing with Jesus' followers).[44] As Paul's trial commences, he apologizes for "reviling" the high priest: "I did not know, brethren, that he was the high priest; for it is written, 'You shall not speak evil of a ruler of your people' " (Acts 23:3-5). Echoing the outcome of Jesus' Sanhedrin trial, no pronouncement of guilt is rendered; the only opinion recorded at all is that of "some of the scribes of the Pharisees' party"[45] indicating that "we find nothing wrong with this man" (Acts 23:9). Later, Luke has Paul resolutely proclaim: "They did not find me disputing with any one or stirring up a crowd, either in the *temple* or in the *synagogue.* . . . They found me purified in the temple. . ." (Acts 24:12, 18); also, "neither against the *law* of the Jews, nor against the *temple* . . . have I offended at all."[46]

In this manner, Luke has driven a wedge between "Judaism" and "Jews." Authentic Judaism has become what Luke's Christianity now is, while Jews who have not accepted Christianity have themselves failed to abide by what was naturally their own legacy! The foregoing series of illustrations may also explain the otherwise unexpected conclusion Luke appends to the pericope of the wineskins. Understood in its natural sense, the new wine may represent Christianity and the old skins, Judaism:

Matt. 9:17	*Mark 2:22*	*Luke 5:37-39*
Neither is new wine put into old wineskins; if it is,	And no one puts new wine into old wineskins; if he does, the wine will	And no one puts new wine into old wineskins; if he does, the new wine will
the skins burst, and the wine is spilled, and the skins are	burst the skins, and the wine is lost, and so are the skins;	burst the skins and it will be spilled, and the skins will be

destroyed; but new wine is put into fresh wineskins, and so both are preserved.

but new wine is for fresh skins.

destroyed. But new wine must be put into fresh wineskins.

And no one after drinking old wine desires new; for he says, "The old is good."

While essentially preserving the Markan pericope, Luke diverts the reader from drawing the natural inference—that the new (Christianity) is incompatible with the old (Judaism), that new matter must take on a completely new form, that new wine must be housed in new skins—by instead sounding a conclusion (Luke 5:39) to the contrary effect: that the old (or old*er*) is "good" (according to some manuscripts, "better"). Here also Luke is attesting that Christianity is the unbroken legatee of the Judaism of the past, that in so far as Christianity extends its elder its own authenticity is thereby affirmed!

Luke and the Motif of Jewish Believers in Acts

It is appropriate at this juncture to evaluate the relevance of this same Lukan concern to problems raised earlier: the significance, in Acts, of Luke's portrait of early successes with thousands of Jews, and of Paul's at least partial successes with them and resumptions of overtures to them. The literary pattern observed by Tyson accounts for these themes in large measure; yet a related matter has thus far remained unclear: what was Luke's overall intent in applying (or allowing) the literary pattern to begin with?

While this motif of success with Jews is unrelated to any Lukan interest in extending the mission into his own time, it is fully consonant with the dozens of illustrations just enumerated. Initial attestations that "myriads" of Jewish believers were attracted to Christianity, followed by recountings of the at least mixed successes by Paul, likewise support Luke's view that Christianity continues and culminates authentic Judaism.

In Luke's day, Christianity's adherents were in the main Gentile. Such a circumstance may not have concerned Luke unduly; himself a Gentile Christian,[47] he may have viewed it as the working out of the divine plan. Indications are, moreover, that Luke found Jewish Christians troublesome in their own right; conceivably, he might not have welcomed any larger a representation.[48] Nonetheless, the conspicuously small number of contemporary Jews accepting Christianity would have constituted a seeming anomaly for some Christians in Luke's day, and may have called for explanation from Luke, even more than from the other Evangelists. For it was Luke in particular who alleged that Christianity's emergence vis-à-vis Judaism had not been a rift, a departure, a breakaway, an abrupt development, but rather a gradual outgrowth, a metamorphosis genuinely extending Judaism. Why, then, were not more Jews accepting a Christianity which, as Luke insisted, was only the natural extension of their own religion?[49]

One answer available to Luke was that, while Christianity's truth was not perceived by Jews in his own day, by no means had it been lost on Jews of a bygone age! For when Christianity had first emerged, discerning and confirming Jews numbered even in the thousands! This, indeed, is what Luke would have us believe.[50] An entirely different reality, however, is more plausible: that not that many Jews were attracted at all; instead, small in number, capturing little attention, the early Christians led only a modest existence.[51] Rather than markedly proliferating in Jewish adherents, developing Christianity began to assume a predominantly Gentile make-up—with Jewish Christians appearing, in a sense, *under*represented[52] already during Paul's ministry. In this view, the "myriads" Luke enlists would be more myth than history.

Supporting this second view is the observation that many traditions in the early chapters of Acts betray both late and Gentile-Christian perspectives, and "cannot possibly [have] come from the primitive community"; they "appear to be primitive only because the New Testament [writer] ascribed them to an earlier period."[53] The genuine Paul, moreover, personally attests both to extensive opposition and opaqueness by Jews to his preachment.[54] His statements on this score—some abrasive, some poignant, some despondent—have the appearance of verisimilitude and should, at the least, caution the reader to be wary of Luke's alternative statistics. The Gospels, meanwhile, though redacted later, yet furnish clues of strong Jewish resistance in the pre-70 C.E. era—and intimate as well some of the specific issues (early?) under dispute.[55] These indications are sometimes set in the context of controversies between scribes/Pharisees and Jesus/disciples (the latter often representing the early church)[56]—and in some cases the original forms of these traditions are demonstrably drawn from pre-Markan collections.[57]

To be sure, it is difficult determining how to date, process, and weigh these evidences of Jewish opposition; moreover, the existence of opposition by some Jews, formidable as it may have been, does not ensure that it effectively prevented other Jews from accepting Christian beliefs. Yet there is no independent corroboration (i.e., other than the Lukan testimony, here disputed) that Jews initially thronged to Christianity. The more compelling thesis is that Luke, by introducing thousands of Jewish believers early on, is, among other possible concerns, attempting to render less disturbing the anomaly of his own day: the peculiar *under*representation of Jews within a Christianity that is alleged to extend Judaism! This recasting, statistically, of Christianity's demographic evolution in effect camouflages[58] the reality that only relatively few Jews had become Christians at any time.[59]

Consistent with this explanation is the progressive reduction, observable in Acts, from (1) initial, considerable success (with thousands: e.g., Acts 2:41-47; 4:4; 5:14; 6:1,7); to (2) only partial or mixed success (13:42-51; 14:1-6; 14:19-22; 17:4-5; 17:10-13); to (3) increasing resistance (18:4-6; 18:12-13; 19:8-9; 21:27-28); to (4) a culminating, final prediction of no success (28:25-28 [". . . this people . . . shall . . . never understand . . . never perceive . . ."]). Such a petering out of success with Jews was essentially predetermined by Luke as a literary means by which gradually to bring his earlier (and unwarrantedly optimistic) "historical" statistics into conformity with the more sobering reality of his own day, by which time the "salvation of God has been sent to the Gentiles," who have proven virtually the only ones then listening (28:28). Now clarified as well are both the tone of finality in the Lukan Paul's denunciations of Jews and its absence when the gospel is rejected by Gentiles! Gentile intransigence (e.g., Acts 19:23-41) would never provoke from the Lukan Paul the kind of scathing castigation reserved for the Jews because, after all, Luke's Christianity is Gentile—and he fashions the words he attributes to Paul very much with this culminating reality in view!

An additional perspective also suggests itself. Here we may find the analogy of a rope to be apt. In some ropes, all strands extend the entire length and are woven and interwoven amongst one another.

Otherwise, if certain strands end earlier, somewhere in midrope, others would have to be introduced to replace them, continuing where they leave off. The result would then be that many strands at rope's end would be other than a natural extension of those at the beginning. In the terms of this analogy, Luke's task was, first, to demonstrate how the Christian rope, Gentile at the completion, was nonetheless also Jewish at the inception; and, second, to explain the process of that transformation—how, when, and why, had the Jewish strands somewhere along the way become intermeshed by and, ultimately, replaced by Gentile strands? Paradoxical as it may sound, as much as Luke needed the presence of Jewish strands in the beginning of the Christian rope, he actually required their absence by the end—to correspond with the reality of Gentile-Christian demography (and practice)[60] in the late first century.

This central issue defines my difference with Tannehill on the matter of a mission to the Jews in Luke's own day. Luke's concern was not to bring more Jews in but plausibly to explain both why the Jewish strands had disappeared and how they had come to be replaced. To aid in this transition, Luke incorporated so-called God-fearers into his narrative—Gentiles who, while remaining such, nonetheless loosely attached themselves to Judaism.[61] In Acts, they function as a literary device[62] serving, to continue the analogy, as transitional fibers. Although Luke would have had us believe that the church was augmented at its very start by thousands of new Jewish believers, he soon needed to integrate masses of Gentiles. To smooth the transition, he used Godfearers as quasi-Jewish Gentiles who could mask the abruptness of the transformation undergone by Christianity's ranks[63]—Godfearers thus precede the incorporation of Gentiles per se who have no ostensible Jewish sympathies whatsoever.

To be sure, Godfearers did exist and attend the synagogue; they are hardly Luke's creation.[64] Rather, his "invention is. . . their immediate and total abandonment of Judaism for Christianity"![65] Artificial as well is their sudden disappearance from Acts! Once "the straight-line picture of the expansion of Christianity . . . run[ning] . . . from the Jews to the Godfearers to the gentiles" has been established by Luke, the Godfearers are not heard from again[66] because, by this late phase of development, a Christianity that is Gentile no longer appears so troubling an anomaly!

One might argue, of course, that in Acts 21 "myriads" of Jewish believers are still being referred to—rather late, given this reconstruction, to find Jews still being introduced! But the myriads in Acts 21 only summarize conversions accomplished before chap. 7. Why (mis)construe them as new myriads when we can "arrive at the sum . . . in 21:20 without the assumption of a single Jewish convert in Jerusalem after 6:7"? It is "not proper to assume . . . that Acts 21:20 refers to . . . additional converts *when that is the very point that needs to be proved!*"[67] Luke indeed himself says as much. Not only is 21:20 set in Jerusalem, but the myriads referred to in this passage must themselves be Judean only—for Luke specifies that these myriads have been told what Paul has been preaching to Diaspora Jews ("the Jews who are among the Gentiles"). In so distinguishing the myriads from the Diaspora context, Luke is identifying them as Judean! And since we know Luke intends to assign Jerusalem and Judean conversions to the early chapters of Acts (as per the plan of 1:8), it is thus confirmed that the "myriads" in Acts 21 refer only to conversions before Acts 7.[68]

It is wise to beware accepting early chapters as normative for a work as a whole![69] The seeming direction of the mission to the Jews embedded in the opening chapters of Acts should not mislead us concerning the narrator's ultimate intention. For Luke's "myth of the 'myriads' " is as artificial as the other devices through which he has associated Jesus, Paul, and Christianity with "things Jewish." If, nonetheless, early chapters are to be cited, it is anti-Jewish passages encountered antecedent to Acts which warrant greater attention. Thus, at the very outset of Jesus' ministry in the Gospel itself, Luke reminds us how Elijah had benefited not Israel but rather the Gentile widow in Sidon, and how Elisha had aided not Israel but another Gentile, Naaman the Syrian.[70] For Luke to have included in the Gospel itself such pointedly pro-Gentile and anti-Jewish intimations, both here and elsewhere[71]—without any concomitant predictions that the Jews would after all eventually join the ranks along with Gentiles (cf. Romans 11)[72]—suggests that "the salvation of the Jews was *never at any time* of any concern to the author of Luke-Acts,"[73] that *from the outset* . . . , unlike Paul, Luke ha[d] abandoned hope of converting Israel . . . , [and the] manifold attempts [in Acts] to throw a bridge between Jews and Christians no longer represent a missionary wooing of Israel: [for] by Luke's time the Christian mission was directed solely to the Gentiles"![74]

Viewed in this light, the Lukan Paul's repeated resumption of overtures to the Jews now appears a device by which Luke can assign responsibility for the underrepresentation of Jews, in Christian ranks, to Jewish intransigence. Had not Paul repeatedly struggled to elicit Jewish interest? Were not his efforts far in excess of all reasonable expectation, given the rebuffs he had endured?[75] Surely, Luke is telling us, only the obstinacy of Jews in the past can account for the reality in the present that Christianity—even though itself the extension of authentic Judaism—is severely underrepresented Jewishly, an eventuality justifying, in Luke's view, the extreme words he ascribes to Jesus: "I tell you, none of those men . . . invited [i.e., the Jews] shall taste my banquet"![76]

II. THE QUESTION OF TRAGIC IRONY

For these reasons, I also differ from Tannehill on his reading of tragic irony in Luke's portrayal of the Jews. We today may view the Jews in Luke-Acts in this fashion—as playing a tragic role— but I feel that, in so doing, we are superimposing our own sensitivities on an author who would hardly himself have shared them! To me, the idea of tragedy, whether ironic or not, requires that the narrator intend to elicit sympathy or empathy from the reader. I do not feel Luke intended to elicit sympathy for the Jews, and certainly do not feel it elicited from me. In Luke-Acts, Jesus, Stephen, and Paul are intended as tragic victims; it is toward *them* that Luke wants our sympathies directed. Regarding the Jews, meanwhile, it is Luke's contention that they receive only what they deserve and what retribution demands.

Ancients fashioning themselves historians were eager to demonstrate how historical events manifest moral meanings.[77] Luke was concerned, in this case, to show that those unjustly opposing Christianity are for that reason rejected, that justice is always requited to evildoers,[78] that those responsible for Jesus' and Stephen's death, while initially excusable for ignorance, are ultimately answerable for their stubborn obstinacy and perversity. The "blood of . . . the prophets . . . [will] be required of" them (Luke 11:50), and not only will "the very stone which the builders rejected . . . become the head of the corner," but "everyone who falls on that stone will be broken to pieces!"[79]

Such sentiments are hardly consonant with any ability on my part to see tragic irony in Luke's portrayal of the Jews—even though I certainly sense it in Paul's feelings in Romans 9–11. We are, after all, in the case of the real Paul, dealing with a Jew deeply despairing and poignantly concerned with those who are his fellow Jews.[80] To the genuine Paul, the blindness of his fellow Jews to the fulfillment of their own heritage is a tragic irony and an ironic tragedy beyond his comprehension.

There is, additionally, still other tragic irony in Romans 11, where Paul is apprehensive that Gentiles would boast and, becoming proud, no longer stand in awe and respect of Jews in their midst (Rom. 11:18ff.)—not only Jews in theory but also Jews in reality, perhaps in Rome itself. The real Paul's apprehension of Gentile attitudes towards Jews ironically and tragically became fulfilled in the person of what some might term his unauthorized biographer, Luke. That indeed is not only ironic; it became tragic for Jews—and for relations between Jews and Christians—throughout history.[81]

8

THE PROBLEM OF JEWISH REJECTION IN ACTS

Joseph B. Tyson

The problem of understanding Luke's treatment of the Jews in Acts is, to a significant extent, one of understanding the ending of Acts and assessing the relationship of the ending to major themes that shape the rest of the book. Almost all scholars agree that the meeting of Paul with Roman Jews (Acts 28:17-28) constitutes a narrative event of special prominence, because of its location in the book of Acts. But some think of this narrative as constituting a special problem, because in it Paul rejects Jews in a way that is incompatible with themes that are worked out in the rest of the book.

The problematic section in Acts is 28:17-28. After the long description of Paul's adventurous sea voyage and his arrival in Rome, we have the final reported incident of the apostle's life.[1] It is significant that, in dealing with the Roman ministry, the only incident that Luke wants to report is one that tells of Paul's relationships with Jews. The section is actually a double one, set on two separate days. The first incident (Acts 28:17-22) occurs three days after Paul arrives in Rome, and the second (28:23-28) at an indefinite time later. In the first, Paul summons a group of Jewish leaders and explains his legal status. The substance of the explanation is that Paul has committed no crimes against Jewish law but was nevertheless accused by Jews and turned over to Roman authorities for trial. Just when the Roman authorities were about to declare him innocent, the Jews objected to the proceedings, and Paul was forced to appeal to Caesar.[2] Paul then says to the Roman Jews that he wants to explain his situation to them since he has been imprisoned "because of the hope of Israel" (28:20). And the Jewish leaders respond that, although they have heard a great deal against the Christian movement, they have not heard anything about Paul and thus are anxious to hear him express his views.

In the second meeting, apparently rank and file Jews, as well as leaders, are present. It is an all-day meeting, in which Paul attempts to convince his hearers about Jesus on the basis of Torah and prophets. The result of the session is that "some were convinced by what he said, while other disbelieved" (Acts 28:24). Then Paul makes one final statement before the group departs. The statement consists of a quotation from Isa. 6:9-10 and an application. The quotation describes Isaiah's contemporaries as lacking in understanding and perception. In Isaiah the description is pronounced by Yahweh, and it functions to predetermine the rejection of the prophet's message. In the application in Acts 28:28, Paul concludes that God's salvation has been sent to the Gentiles, who will listen and presumably accept it. The perceptive reader of Acts will recognize that the solemn announcement in 28:28 is a repetition of one made on two occasions in the past, in Acts 13:46 and 18:6.

There has recently been a great deal of discussion about the intended meaning of this concluding section of Acts and its bearing on Luke's treatment of the Jews. Jacob Jervell maintains that Luke has, at the end of Acts, declared an end to the Jewish mission but not because it was a failure.[3] On the contrary, according to Jervell Luke shows that the Gentile mission can begin because the Jewish mission was a success. The quotation from Isaiah in Acts 28:26-27 is directed against the unrepentant Jews and is not in conflict with 28:24, which distinguishes between the repentant and the unrepentant. Jervell calls attention to the similarities between the description of Paul's mission in Rome and many earlier narratives, in which a distinction is made between those Jews who accept the Christian message and those who do not. The result of Paul's preaching in Rome is both positive and negative, as it had been all along. Robert Tannehill thinks that the ending of Acts does not categorically mark the end of the mission to the Jews.[4] Although, after the end of the Acts narrative, the church's work will be predominantly among Gentiles, Jews are always to be welcomed into Christian fellowship. He observes that in the concluding summary statement in Acts 28:30,

Paul welcomes *all* who come to him and continues to preach to them about Jesus and the kingdom. Tannehill insists that "all" in Acts 28:30 must include Jews as well as Gentiles.

Other scholars, however, have taken an opposite view, namely, that in Acts, Luke narrates a failed mission to the Jews, the termination of which is announced in Acts 28:28.[5]

The failure of modern scholars to agree about the meaning of these verses in Acts suggests that Luke's presentation may be complex. Although there are a number of exegetical problems in Acts 28:17-28, the major one appears to be the inappropriateness of Paul's concluding remarks.[6] These words reflect the view that the mission to Jews has been a failure and announce the termination of that mission. In a quite literal sense, these remarks appear to be inappropriate to the situation. Although Paul applies Isaiah's condemnation to Jews generally, some of his Jewish hearers have accepted his message. It does not help to say that the condemnation applies only to those who did not accept Paul's message, although logic may demand that interpretation. The quotation speaks of the people *(ho laos)*. It is the people who lack understanding and perception, whose hearing is defective and whose eyes have closed. As Nils Dahl has shown, the term *ho laos* in Luke-Acts almost always applies to the Jewish people, and Luke clearly understands the quotation from Isaiah to refer to them (cf. "your fathers" in 28:25).[7] This understanding is particularly compelling when we relate the quotation to its application in Acts 28:28, which implicitly contrasts the expected attitude of Gentiles with the lack of understanding and perception found among Jews.

But there is one condition under which Paul's concluding words may be appropriate. If we should proceed from the view that the acceptance that is mentioned in Acts 28:24 is, for Luke, an example of individual Jewish response, while the rejection in 28:25-28 designates the corporate Jewish response, we would be in a position to understand the passage as internally consistent. Under this view, there is a fundamental distinction between the collective response of Jews as a whole and the response of individual Jews. Given this distinction, we may then say that, although Luke feels that any positive response from individual Jews should be noted and celebrated, that response is not sufficient, since what is intended is the conversion of the people as a whole and that, since this wholesale conversion has not occurred, the Pauline mission will hereafter be directed toward Gentiles. The passage leaves no hint that there will be a return to the Jewish mission, and it gives every indication that the previous mission to the Jews, which Luke has so abundantly described, has been a failure.

This way of understanding the passage calls attention to a certain tension and ambivalence in Luke's presentation in regard to the Jewish people. There seems to be no hesitancy in reporting that some of Paul's Jewish hearers responded positively, nor any reluctance to condemn the Jews as a whole for their rejection of Paul's message. Indeed, this ambivalence is characteristic of Luke's presentation throughout the book of Acts, as we shall see in dealing with certain objections to the interpretation suggested above.[8]

At least three major objections to our interpretation must be faced. One objection is that Luke seems to have such a deep interest in Jewish religious traditions that it is inconceivable that he would ever think that the mission to Jews was over. Another objection is that, since Luke has so much material about the conversion of individual Jews and the important role they played in the life of the church, it is incorrect to think that their conversion is insufficient. A third objection is that, since Luke devotes a great deal of attention to the story of the church in Jerusalem, it is impossible to think that, in his eyes, the existence of this corporate Jewish-Christian body is an insufficient fulfillment of the mission to the Jews.

LUKE'S INTEREST IN JEWISH RELIGIOUS TRADITIONS

Luke-Acts manifests a number of paradoxes, and among them is the treatment of Jews and Gentiles. It has often been observed that the Lukan writings impel the reader toward sympathy with the Gentile mission. From first to last, the Christian movement seems headed in the direction of Gentiles. The first sermon of Jesus in Nazareth (Luke 4:16-30) announces this point, as do several indicators in the book of Acts.[9] Despite this programmatic theme in Luke-Acts, the author displays much more interest in Jews than he does in Gentiles. There are, after all, very few references to Gentile religious traditions in Acts. At a few points, Luke calls attention to Gentile polytheism, most markedly in Acts 17. Here we have a speech of Paul that begins with an observation about Gentile polytheism and uses this observation to proclaim a monotheistic faith (Acts 17:22-31). Similarly, the attempt on the part of the citizens of Lystra to worship Barnabas as Zeus and Paul as Hermes reflects a polytheism in which gods may appear as human beings (14:8-18). Perhaps the most dramatic scene that displays an interest in Gentile religious traditions is in Acts 19:23-41. Here opposition to Paul and his associates arises from Demetrius and those who make silver shrines to the goddess Artemis. Although Luke seems intent on showing that the opposition sprang from a perceived threat to Demetrius's livelihood, there are reflections in the narrative of religious devotion. Fear is expressed that Paul's preaching will discredit the Temple of Artemis (19:27), and crowds shout, "Great is Artemis of the Ephesians!" (19:28, 34).

But this information pales into insignificance when compared with the rich detail in both Luke and Acts about Jewish religious traditions. Luke has a deep interest in the temple and in Torah observance. He knows about Passover and Pentecost.[10] He is interested in the differences between Pharisees and Sadducees, the role of priests, chief priests, scribes, and elders.[11] There is in Luke-Acts a host of details about hours of prayer (Acts 3:1; 10:30-31) and about the furniture of the temple (Luke 1:11), its gates (Acts 3:2, 10) and porticoes (Acts 3:11; 5:12). Luke knows of the importance of Sabbath observance and of the place of synagogues in Jewish communities. There are abundant references to Hebrew prophets (Joel, Isaiah, Samuel), kings (Saul, David, Solomon), patriarchs (Abraham, Isaac, Jacob), and leaders (Moses, Aaron, Joshua), as well as quotations from the Hebrew Scriptures.

Perhaps the amount of detail about Jewish religious traditions is due simply to the setting of the narrative. The locus of the Gospel and over half of Acts is, of course, predominantly Jewish territory. But in the sections of Acts that are set in Gentile territory, no such detailed interest in Gentile religious traditions is to be found. Indeed, even in many sections set in Gentile lands, we find references to Jewish synagogues and places of prayer. Even considering the setting, Luke's interest in things Jewish exceeds what is necessary for narrative realism.

Luke's interest probably roots in his understanding of the relationship between the Christian message and the Jewish people. It is not without significance that the Christian preachers frequently speak in terms that identify them with their Jewish audience. They speak of "our fathers," to designate not only Abraham, Isaac, and Jacob, but also past generations of Jews. At his trials, Paul more than once emphasizes his Jewish heritage. At one point he defines Christian theology as worshiping "the God of our fathers, believing everything laid down by the law or written in the prophets, [and] having a hope in God which these themselves accept, that there will be a resurrection of both the just and the unjust" (Acts 24:14-15). Of course, Luke is aware that not all Jews accept the belief in the resurrection, but on the other points he insists on an identity between Christian and Jewish religion. At several points Paul and other speakers struggle to explain the relationship between the Hebrew Scriptures and Jesus.[12] For Luke, there is a continuity between the Scriptures and the Christian message, and this sense of continuity largely accounts for the deep interest that he displays in Jewish religious traditions.[13]

But the sense of continuity creates a serious problem, and Luke's clear interest in Jewish traditions creates for him a deep tension. Although for Luke the proclamation about Jesus comes from Jewish preachers and is intended for a Jewish audience, and although it is consistent with Jewish religious traditions and with the Hebrew Scriptures, the Jews have rejected it.

This is precisely the problem in the closing section of Acts, where Paul speaks of "our fathers" (28:17), explains that he has been imprisoned because of "the hope of Israel" (28:20), preaches to his Jewish audience from "the law of Moses and from the prophets" (28:23), but still announces that the Jews have rejected the message (28:28). Indeed, one may find a small clue to a significant change in this section. In the first meeting of Paul with the Jewish leaders in Rome, he speaks of "the customs of our fathers" (28:17), but at the end of the second meeting he speaks of "your fathers" (28:25) as those condemned by Isaiah. The different pronouns indicate a subtle distancing of Paul from the Jews, who have rejected his preaching.

The objection that Luke has a deep interest in things Jewish cannot be met by denying it, but the interest itself does not determine the question of Jewish acceptance or rejection. His interest in Jewish religious traditions and in the continuity between Judaism and Christianity does not prevent him from concluding that the mission to Jews was a failure, since Jews as a whole had rejected the Christian preaching. His interest does, however, add poignancy to his narrative. For Luke, rejection by Jews has not occurred because the Christian message was incomprehensible to them or incompatible with their traditions. On the contrary, Jewish rejection occurred despite the fact that the Christian message was harmonious with Jewish religious traditions. Thus Luke's narrative is replete with an irony that probably originated in the author's own tension and ambivalence.

THE ROLE OF JEWISH BELIEVERS

The second objection that may be made to the contention that Luke finally regards the mission to the Jews as a failure is that his narrative in Acts features the part played by a number of individual Jewish believers. Not only are there successful missions in almost every locality that Paul and his associates visit, but also the real heroes of Acts are those preachers and missionaries who were, or are, Jews. The point is so obvious that it needs no elaboration, except to call attention to the stories about Peter, Philip, Stephen, Paul, and others. This fact is stressed when Paul twice states to his captors and opponents, "I am a Jew" (Acts 21:39; 22:3), and when he proclaims to the Sanhedrin, "I am a Pharisee" (23:6). It is significant that in all three of these statements the verb is in the present tense. At the time these announcements are made, the Lukan Paul sees no inconsistencies between his belief in Jesus and his status as a Jew. Indeed, the Christian and Pharisaic agreement on belief in resurrection is stressed in Acts 23. It is also worth observing that there are no Christian leaders in Acts who are clearly designated as Gentiles. The most notable Gentile Christian is Cornelius, and he is treated chiefly as a recipient of the gospel through the Jewish-Christian apostle Peter.

One aspect of the role of Peter, Paul, and the others is to demonstrate the Lukan theme of continuity between Judaism and Christianity. Their stories are absolutely necessary to provide flesh to the Lukan theme. Indeed, this fact adds poignancy and irony to Luke's presentation. Christianity is not in conflict with Judaism, and the chief representatives of the Christian movement are themselves Jews who demonstrate this harmony. But the point to be stressed is that, despite the model roles of these Jewish believers, the Jews have rejected the Christian message. Peter, Stephen, and Paul are individual Jews, and there is a significant difference between the conversion of these individuals and the conversion of Jews as a whole.

A tell-tale sign of this difference may be seen in the different ways in which Luke uses the singular *Jew* and the plural *Jews*. *Ioudaios* in the singular is found only 10 times in Acts. Two appearances have already been observed, viz., Acts 21:39; 22:3, where Paul announces that he is a Jew. One reference appears in a general statement of principle, viz., 10:28, where Peter states that it is unlawful for a Jew to visit with a Gentile. All the rest are used in the identification of particular persons of various characters. Bar-Jesus, the Jewish false prophet (13:6), is an opponent of Paul, and Sceva, the Jewish high priest (19:14), attempts to misuse the name of Jesus. Drusilla, the wife of Felix (24:24), is identified as a Jewish woman, but she is not an active character in the narrative. The others who are identified as Jewish individuals are sympathetic, or at least quasi-sympathetic characters. Timothy, who became an associate of Paul, is identified as the son of a Jewish woman (16:1). Aquila (18:2) was an associate of Paul. Apollos (18:24), after instruction from Priscilla and Aquila, became a powerful spokesperson for the Christians. Alexander (19:34) apparently would have been a defender of Paul in Ephesus, if he had been allowed to speak. Thus, Luke usually uses the term "Jew" in the singular to designate a specific person, and the word itself does not carry any pejorative value.[14]

The case is quite different with the use of the term in the plural, which occurs some 69 times. Although it is frequently used in a neutral sense, to describe Jewish customs, to designate Jewish synagogues, or simply to speak of the Jewish people, the characteristic and most striking uses are those that speak collectively of Jews as opponents. They plot to kill Saul (9:23); they plan some punishment for Peter (12:11); they are filled with jealousy against Paul (13:45; 17:5); they incite others (13:50; 14:19); they come from Thessalonica to Beroea to oppose Paul (17:13); they attack Paul in Corinth (18:12); and they plot against him in Greece (20:3). Jewish opposition to Paul reaches its zenith after he returns to Jerusalem for the last time. In contrast to the trials of Jesus in the Gospel of Luke, where the major opposition comes from the chief priests, the chief opponents of Paul in Acts are simply the Jews.[15] The Jews incite riots (21:27), plot against him (23:12), and accuse him before Roman authorities (22:30; 24:9; 25:7,24; 26:2,7). The distinction between the singular and the plural uses of the term *Jew* is striking. While the singular may designate an individual, either helper or opponent, the plural characteristically refers to opponents.[16] Stephen's condemnation seems intended for the corporate body of Jews as a whole: "You stiff-necked people, uncircumcised in heart and ears, you always resist the Holy Spirit. As your fathers did, so do you" (Acts 7:51).[17]

This distinction provides some insight into the exegetical problem posed by the closing section of the book. The chief problem in this passage is that Paul appears to condemn general Jewish rejection of his message even in the face of acceptance of the message by some Jews. But this is a problem not only in the closing section of Acts. The distinction between Luke's attitude toward individual Jews and toward Jews as a whole is exhibited not only in the closing section of Acts but is to be found in the language of the entire book.

The problem encountered in Acts 28:17-28 is also to be found in a number of earlier pericopes in Acts, where the situation is the same. In Pisidian Antioch, Paul begins his mission by preaching in the synagogue, upon invitation from the leaders. The result of the preaching is that "many Jews and devout converts to Judaism followed Paul and Barnabas, who spoke to them and urged them to continue in the grace of God" (13:43). On the next Sabbath, however, the Jews "were filled with jealousy, and contradicted what was spoken by Paul, and reviled him" (13:45). Immediately following is the first of the three announcements that speak of the end of the Jewish mission and the beginning of the Gentile: "It was necessary that the word of God should be spoken first to you. Since you thrust it from you, and judge yourselves unworthy of eternal life, behold, we turn to the Gentiles" (13:46).

At Iconium a group of both Jews and Greeks accepted the Christian message, but "unbelieving Jews stirred up the Gentiles and poisoned their minds against the brethren" (14:2). Here it is notable that the distinction between believing and unbelieving Jews is maintained. But a few sentences later, in 14:4, a different division is observed among the citizens of Iconium: "some sided with the Jews, and some with the apostles" (14:4).

The situation in Thessalonica is terminologically less clear. Here Paul and Silas preach in the synagogue, "and some of *them* were persuaded, and joined Paul and Silas; as did a great many of the devout Greeks and not a few of the leading women" (17:4). The italicized pronoun must refer to Jews, i.e., the ones addressed in the synagogue. Thus 17:4 would refer to the conversion of some Jews, many Greeks, and not a few leading women, presumably also Gentiles. But in the following verse, Luke observes that "the Jews were jealous" and that they incited a riot.

There is some variation in the narrative about Beroea. The Jews there accept Paul's message, but the Jews from Thessalonica come down to oppose it (17:10-15). In Corinth, although Aquila persuades Jews and Greeks (18:4), Jews oppose Paul, who, for the second time, announces the end of the Jewish mission (18:6).

We may appropriately speak of a literary pattern in Acts that, with some variation, includes the following elements: preaching in a synagogue; acceptance of the Christian message by some Jews and Gentiles; opposition from the Jews. In this pattern, Luke does not seem to be concerned with what appears to be a logical inconsistency. Acceptance of the Christian message by some Jews does not minimize the impact of the rejection by Jews as a whole.

Thus, the objection that Luke has a deep interest in the work of individual Jews, such as Peter and Paul, does not hold up. Their work, remarkable as it is, does not form an exception to the overwhelming phenomenon of Jewish rejection and does not diminish Luke's sense of the failure of the Jewish mission. Individual acceptance and corporate rejection stand side by side in Luke's narrative.

THE JEWISH CHRISTIANS IN JERUSALEM

Although it has become customary in modern scholarship to use the term "Jewish Christian," it is notable that Luke never uses it. Indeed, the term "Christian" appears only twice (Acts 11:26; 26:28). The closest Luke comes to our nomenclature is in a reference by James to those "among the Jews who have believed" (Acts 21:20). It is significant that Luke has no simple terminology to call attention to believing Jews.

Nevertheless, Luke is clearly aware that there was a large group of Jewish believers. The first major section of Acts is devoted to a series of narratives about these believers, and Luke even emphasizes the numerical growth in the community in Jerusalem.[18] Acts 1:4—8:3 is almost idyllic in its description of this community. Luke emphasizes its harmony, the sharing of possessions, the obedience of the disciples to the apostles, the common rituals, and the spiritual power manifested in healing miracles.[19] Despite the problems with the Jewish leaders, these believers and the apostles are held in high regard by the people of Jerusalem.

The harmony associated with the beginning of the Jerusalem community, however, does not continue. Some members are not obedient to the requirement to donate proceeds from the sale of property to the apostles (Acts 5:1-11). Disputes arise about distributions to Hebrew and Hellenistic widows (6:1-6). After the execution of Stephen, a persecution arises that results in the scattering of the church, except for the apostles (8:1). But the author has not finished with the Jerusalem church. Attention to it returns on three major occasions in the course of the narrative. These three occasions should now be examined.

The first return of attention to Jerusalem is in Acts 11. In the previous chapter Luke has gone into great detail to describe a vision of Peter and the baptism of Cornelius and his household. The amount of space that he spends on this narrative, as well as on the visionary and miraculous elements in it, suggests its importance for the author. It marks a major transition in the Acts narrative, namely, the initiation of the Gentile mission. But something stands in the way of this mission, and the vision of Peter is intended to signify the removal of this barrier. The barrier has been understood by some to be the unclean state of Gentiles.[20] But it is probably nearer the truth to say that the barrier, as Luke understands it, is the inhibition of social relations between Jews and Gentiles caused by the Jewish dietary regulations.[21] Peter's vision is effectively the annulment of the dietary regulations of Leviticus: the voice from heaven declares clean the foods that Jews, such as Peter, have traditionally avoided eating.[22] Thus the way is open for Peter to visit with Cornelius, and he does so. The centurion and his household are baptized and receive the

Spirit, as did the original apostles in Acts 2. All this takes place outside of Jerusalem, in Joppa and Caesarea. But when Peter returns to Jerusalem, he is met with opposition from "the circumcision party" (Acts 11:2). These critics ask why Peter visited and ate with uncircumcised men. So Peter retells the story of his vision and his dealings with Cornelius, after which those in Jerusalem say, "Then to the Gentiles also God has granted repentance unto life" (11:18).

Although the story of Cornelius ends with an agreement between Peter and the others in Jerusalem, we must not overlook the controversial character of the last part of the narrative. Those who make up the opposition to Peter, the circumcision party, are not unbelieving Jews, but Christians. This means that Luke wants the reader to know about the presence among the Jewish Christians in Jerusalem of certain ones who attempted to resist the Spirit. That they are silenced by Peter's report may appear to be conclusive, but in fact their silence is only temporary.

The second incident involving controversy among the Jewish Christians in Jerusalem is found in Acts 15. Controversy here is over the requirement of circumcision for Gentile Christians, a controversy not restricted to Jerusalem, but precipitated by persons from Judea (cf. 15:1,24). These people are designated by Luke as "believers who belonged to the party of the Pharisees" (Acts 15:5), but they seem to play the same role that the members of the "circumcision party" played in Acts 11:2. They preach that "it is necessary to circumcise them [the Gentile believers], and to charge them to keep the law of Moses" (15:5; cf. 15:1). This controversy is settled when Paul and Barnabas meet in Jerusalem with Peter, James, the other apostles, and the elders. The decision, announced by James, is not to require circumcision or full Torah obedience, but rather only to require abstention from idolatry and unchastity, and avoidance of blood and of things strangled (15:20). As in the Cornelius narrative, so here, the fact that some settlement of the problem was achieved should not cause us to neglect the fact that the problem did arise and arose specifically because the Jerusalem church included some who resisted alteration of Jewish religious traditions and inhibited the mission to the Gentiles. Thus far, this element in the church has not had the upper hand, but in the third incident, things seem to have changed.

The third incident is found in Acts 21. After Paul returns to

Jerusalem for the last time, he meets with James and the elders, who hear his report of missionary work among the Gentiles and glorify God. But then James informs Paul about certain feelings harbored by the Jerusalem Christians. He says, "You see, brother, how many thousands there are among the Jews of those who have believed; they are all zealous for the law, and they have been told about you that you teach all the Jews who are among the Gentiles to forsake Moses, telling them not to circumcise their children or observe the customs" (Acts 21:20-21). The Lukan James makes it clear that these anti-Pauline charges are false; nevertheless, he thinks that it is necessary to give the opponents some visible demonstration that Paul has not forsaken the traditions. Thus the plan is made for Paul to purify himself ritually and support the religious expenses of four pious men. In a certain respect, this narrative is more disturbing than the others. It suggests not only that there is Christian opposition to Paul but also that it is powerful, so powerful that it is necessary for the leaders of the church to grant concessions.[23] Moreover, here is no controversy that can be settled by discussion and agreement. The opposition must be ameliorated by some symbolic demonstration.

But there is nothing in Acts that would suggest that there was any settlement of the controversy, nothing to indicate that Paul's Christian opponents understood or appreciated his symbolic gesture. In the following narratives, which describe the opposition to Paul from the Jews, no mention is made of any fellow Christians in Jerusalem. This is a surprising result when we recall the power and harmony of this community as described in the early chapters of Acts and when we consider the size of it as reported in Acts 21:20. The contrast is dramatic, since the last we hear of Christians in Jerusalem involves shattering disharmony and incredible impotence.

It cannot be denied that Luke has a deep interest in the very earliest community of Christians in Jerusalem. But his references to this group of Jewish-Christian believers in Chaps. 11, 15, and 21 suggest a progressive deterioration of the community and, subsequently, a loss of narrative relevance. To be sure, the numbers of believers among the Jews in Jerusalem do not shrink, but there appears to be a progressive reorientation, as if the community sank back into a reactionary position that could not be distinguished from the Jewish traditions of the nonbelievers. This does not mean that the Jewish

Christians of Jerusalem became insignificant to Luke, but it is to say that the existence of this community does not, for him, create an exception to the final failure of the Jewish mission and the Jewish rejection of the gospel.

CONCLUSION

Luke's treatment of the Jewish Christians is symptomatic of his deep ambivalence, as we see it demonstrated in the conclusion to Acts. Here we see the tension between his condemnation of Jewish rejection and his description of Jewish acceptance. In the final analysis it appears that Jewish acceptance is less important to him than Jewish rejection. Or, to put it differently, he can only speak of a partial Jewish acceptance—and that is not enough. Thus, even the part finally becomes irrelevant. To be sure, near the end of his narrative he can speak of myriads of believers from among the Jews but, on examination, these Jewish Christians turn out to be counted among the opponents, not among the heroes. The important thing about them is not that they are believers but that they oppose Paul.

The book of Acts might, thus, appropriately be titled, "The Problem of Jewish Rejection." This is not to suggest that we should neglect the importance of his emphasis on the Gentile mission. This is simply the other side of the same coin. Nevertheless, since this author displays so much more interest in Jewish than in Gentile religious traditions, it is appropriate to think of him as more concerned about Jews than about Gentiles. The problem of Jewish rejection is finally more significant than the story of Gentile acceptance. This too shows his ambivalence. While he ends with Paul preaching the gospel in Rome, "openly and unhindered" (Acts 28:31), not far from his mind is the rejection by that final group of Jews that Paul tried to convince. It is impossible to know what emotional quality might be present as this author completed his work. He seems not overly triumphalist in writing about Paul among Gentiles in Rome, nor does he seem shattered by his realization that the mission to Jews has been a failure. But two facts seem clear: for Luke the mission to the Jewish people has failed, and it has been terminated.

NOTES

Chapter 1. Jacob Jervell, "The Church of Jews and Godfearers"

1. The terminology used by Luke to denote the Godfearers in Acts is (a) *phoboumenos*, 10:2, 22, 35; 13:16, 26; (b) *eusebēs, sebomenos*, 10:2, 7; 13:43, 50; 16:14; 17:4, 17; 18:7; and (c) *Hellēn*, 11:20; 14:1; 17:4; 18:4; 19:10, 17; 20:21; 21:28.
2. Cf. Jacob Jervell, "The History of Early Christianity and the Acts of the Apostles," in *The Unknown Paul* (Minneapolis: Augsburg, 1984), pp. 13-25.
3. For material about Godfearers in Judaism cf. *CII*, especially 1:495; Lit.: Heinz Bellen, *"Synagōge tōn ioudaiōn kai theosebōn.* Die Aussage einer bosporanischen Freilassungsinschrift (CIRB 71) zum Problem der 'Gottesfürchtigen,' " *JAC* 8-9 (1965–1966): 171-176; Franz Bömer, *Untersuchungen über die Religion der Sklaven in Griechenland und Rom* (Mainz: Akademie der Wissenschaften und der Literatur, 1958–1963), 2:101-106; John G. Gager, "Jews, Gentiles, and Synagogues in the Book of Acts," *HTR* 79 (1986): 91-99; A. Thomas Kraabel, "The Disappearance of the 'Godfearers,' " *Numen* 28 (1981): 113-126; idem, "Greeks, Jews, and Lutherans in the Middle Half of Acts," *HTR* 79 (1986): 147-157; B. Lifshitz, "Du nouveau sur les 'Sympathisants,' " *JSJ* 1 (1970): 77-84; K. Romaniuk, "Die 'Gottesfürchtigen' im Neuen Testament," *Aegyptus* 1-2 (1964): 66-91; W. Schrage, *"Synagōgē,"* *TWNT* (1964) 7:824. For the latest evidence on the inscription from ancient Aphrodisia, cf. Gager, "Synagogues," pp. 97f.
4. The Godfearers are far more than "sympathizers."
5. To the Jews, the Gentile who worships God in connection with the synagogue has a different status from that of the "ordinary" Gentile; so K. G. Kuhn, *"Prosēlytos,"* *TWNT* (1959) 6:741.
6. This is the view of Luke. But you can find the same idea in Jewish sources; cf. Josephus, *War* 7:43-53; see Adolf von Harnack, *The Mission and Expansion of Christianity in the First Three Centuries*, 2nd ed., trans. and ed. James Moffatt (London: Williams and Norgate; New York: G. P. Putnam's Sons, 1908) 1:17; Gustav Adolf Deissmann, *Licht vom Osten: Das Neuen Testament und die neuentdecken Texte der hellenistich-römischen Welt*, 4th ed. (Tübingen: J. C. B. Mohr, 1923), pp. 392f.; Gager, "Synagogues"; Emil Schürer, "Die siebentägige Woche im Gebräuche der christlichen Kirche der ersten Jahrhunderte," *ZNW* 6 (1905): 40ff.
7. Cf. especially Kraabel, "Godfearers," and "Greeks, Jews, and Lutherans."

8. The synagogal community included even the Godfearers: Bellen, *"Synagōgē,"* pp. 170ff.; Str-B, 2:715. "Godfearer" is a title of honor and tells something about how these people were evaluated, cf. Lifshitz, "Sympathisants," p. 82.

9. So goes the opinion even in Jewish sources, in spite of the fact that some contempt for proselytes is expressed in certain later periods. In Tannaitic times some suggested that proselytes should not be forced to undergo circumcision, but that baptism was sufficient; cf. *y.Bik.* 1:4:64a; *b.Yebam.* 46a, 48b; *b.Ned.* 32a; Michael Avi-Yonah, *Geschichte der Juden im Zeitalter des Talmud in den Tagen von Rom und Byzanz,* Studia Judaica; Forschungen zur Wissenschaft des Judentums 2 (Berlin: de Gruyter, 1962), pp. 82f.; *Sib. Or.* 4:164; Josephus, *Ant.* 20:38-42.

10. Cf. Klaus Berger, "Almösen für Israel: Zum Historischen Kontext der Paulinischen Kollekte," *NTS* 23 (1977): 192.

11. Cf. H. Balz, *"Phobeō,"* *TDNT* (1974) 9:213: The conversion of Cornelius is "strictly the winning of a marginal member of the Jewish community for the Christian community."

12. Ernst Haenchen, *The Acts of the Apostles: A Commentary,* trans. Bernard Noble, et. al. (Philadelphia: Westminster, 1971), sees that 10:35 has to do with Godfearers, but he adds: "without excluding others." So Haenchen forces upon Luke his own ideas about the Gentile mission.

13. Cf. Berger, "Almösen," pp. 183f.

14. Cf. Jacob Jervell, *Luke and the People of God* (Minneapolis: Augsburg, 1972), pp. 44ff.

15. The synagogal community consisted of Jews as well as of Godfearers; see note 8 above. On the inscription at Miletus, see Bellen, *"Synagōgē,"* pp. 171ff.; Deissmann, *Licht vom Osten,* p. 392; Lifshitz, "Sympathisants," p. 172: "Les 'sympathisants' ne prevaient pas manger avec les Hellenes ni—cela va de soi—participer a leurs banquets."

16. "Greeks," *hellēnas,* are to Luke Godfearers; cf. Kuhn, *"Prosēlytos,"* p. 741; cf. K. G. Kuhn and H. Stegemann, "Proselyten," *PWSup* (1962) 9:1248-1283.

17. Acts 11:20 is talking about Godfearers. Cf. Kuhn and Stegemann, "Proselyten."

18. Cf. Kuhn, *"Prosēlytos,"* p. 744.

19. Cf. Jervell, "The Center of Scripture in Luke," trans. Roy A. Harrisville, in *The Unknown Paul,* pp. 122-137.

20. Cf. my forthcoming essay, "Das Aposteldekret in der lukanischen Theologie."

21. Luke is often more rigid in his claims upon Gentiles than they often were in the Jewish mission; cf. Emil Schürer, *Geschichte des jüdischen Volkes im zeitalter Jesus Christi* (Leipzig: J. C. Hinrichs, 1898–1902) 3:102ff.

22. Cf. Kuhn, *"Prosēlytos,"* p. 744; Kuhn and Stegemann, "Proselyten," p. 1282; Balz, *"Phobeō,"* p. 213, n. 128.

23. Cf. Kuhn, *"Prosēlytos,"* p. 744.

24. In the Gospel of Luke *ta ethnē* has only negative connotations; cf. Luke 12:30; 18:32; 21:24; 22:25.

25. For a different view cf. Alfons Weiser, *Die Apostelgeschichte,* Ökumenischer Taschenbuchkommentar zum Neuen Testament 5 (Gütersloh: Gütersloher Verlaghaus Gerd Mohn; Würzburg: Echter-Verlag, 1981–1985) 2:253; He points to Acts 14:20 as talking about the disciples in Lystra. But this is not connected to the episode and only says that Luke knew about Christians in Lystra.

26. Cf. Gerd Lüdemann, *Das frühe Christentum nach den Traditionen der Apostelgeschichte* (Göttingen: Vandenhoeck & Ruprecht, 1987), p. 198.

27. Hans Conzelmann, *Die Apostelgeschichte* (Tübingen: J. C. B. Mohr [Paul Siebeck], 1963), p. 96; Martin Dibelius, *Aufsätze zur Apostelgeschichte*, 5th ed. Heinrich Greeven (Göttingen: Vandenhoeck & Ruprecht, 1986), p. 61; Jürgen Roloff, *Die Apostelgeschichte*, NTD 5 (Göttingen: Vandenhoeck & Ruprecht, 1981), p. 257; Gustav Stählin, *Die Apostelgeschichte*, 7th ed., NTD 5 (Göttingen: Vandenhoeck & Ruprecht, 1980), p. 228.

28. The tension is mostly seen, but left without any explanation, in the commentaries; cf. e.g., Conzelmann, Haenchen, Stählin, Weiser, and Schneider; cf. also Dibelius, *Aufsätze zur Apostelgeschichte*, p. 66.

29. Cf. Roloff, *Apostelgeschichte*, p. 257.

30. Cf Jervell, *Luke and the People of God*, pp. 41-74.

31. Cf. ibid., pp. 133-151.

32. Cf. Jervell, "The Mighty Minority," in *The Unknown Paul*, pp. 26-51.

Chapter 2. David L. Tiede, " 'Glory to Thy People Israel': Luke-Acts and the Jews"

1. See Robert L. Wilken, *The Myth of Christian Beginnings* (Garden City, N.Y.: Doubleday, 1971).

2. Popular Christian preaching has long been permeated with such claims, but scholarly interpretations have often supported these views on historical grounds with or without intention. See Ernst Haenchen, "The Book of Acts as Source Material for the History of Early Christianity," in *Studies in Luke-Acts*, ed. Leander E. Keck and J. Louis Martyn (Nashville: Abingdon, 1966), p. 278: "Luke has written the Jews off."

3. See Charlotte Klein, *Anti-Judaism in Christian Theology*, trans. Edward Quinn (Philadelphia: Fortress, 1978).

4. A burgeoning scholarship on Luke-Acts is ample testimony to the wide diversity of approaches and contributions which could be mentioned. In the 1950s and 1960s, Hans Conzelmann's *The Theology of St. Luke*, trans. Geoffrey Buswell (New York: Harper and Brothers, 1960) actually intensified the traditional view of Luke on the Jews with its historical schematization, and the note of Gentile triumph at Jewish expense was explored further and criticized in the interpretations of Vielhauer, Käsemann, and Haenchen. Among the many challenges to this consensus, the most controversial and influential has been Jacob Jervell's essay, "The Divided People of God," in *Luke and the People of God: A New Look at Luke-Acts* (Minneapolis: Augsburg, 1972), pp. 41-74. See also Augustin George, "Israel dans l'oeuvre de Luc," *RB* 75 (1968): 481-525; Joseph B. Tyson, "The Jewish Public in Luke-Acts," *NTS* 30 (1984):574-583.

5. George Foot Moore's classic study, *Judaism*, 3 vols. (Cambridge: Harvard University Press, 1927–1930), established the concept of "normative Judaism," which was well received by both modern Christianity and Judaism as each sought to trace its tradition to some clear wellspring of heritage. Now the origins of both formative Christianity and formative Judaism appear much more complex and interconnected with a broader range of Jewish traditions in the Greco-Roman era. See Jacob Neusner's clear discussion of these broad issues in *Judaism in the Beginning of Christianity* (Philadelphia: Fortress, 1984). See especially p. 10: "The catalytic event in the formation of the kind of Judaism we now know as normative—that is, the Judaism that took shape in the documents produced by rabbis from the first through the seventh centuries—was

the destruction of the Temple in 70 C.E. That same event proved decisive in the formation of Christianity as an autonomous and self-conscious community of Israelite faith." See also Jacob Jervell's assessment of the place of the Gentile mission in the late first century, "The History of Early Christianity and the Acts of the Apostles," in *The Unknown Paul: Essays on Luke-Acts and Early Christian History* (Minneapolis: Augsburg, 1984), pp. 13-25.

6. Jack T. Sanders has made the fascinating suggestion that "the Pharisees in the Gospel are the prototypes of the Christian Pharisees in Acts 15:5 who likewise advise that those desiring admission to the church should strictly follow the Law of Moses and not rely on their 'belief' to get in" ("The Pharisees in Luke-Acts," in *The Living Text: Essays in Honor of Ernest W. Saunders,* ed. Dennis E. Groh and Robert Jewett [New York: University Press of America, 1985], p. 181).

7. See Norman R. Petersen, *Literary Criticism for New Testament Critics* (Philadelphia: Fortress, 1978), p. 83; and David L. Tiede, *Prophecy and History in Luke-Acts* (Philadelphia: Fortress, 1980).

8. See David L. Tiede, "The Exaltation of Jesus and the Restoration of Israel in Acts 1," *HTR* 79 (1986):278-286.

9. Henry J. Cadbury, *The Making of Luke-Acts* (London: SPCK, 1927); See also Cadbury, *The Style and Literary Method of Luke,* HTS 6 (Cambridge: Harvard University Press, 1920).

10. See Martin Dibelius, "The Speeches in Acts and Ancient Historiography," in *Studies in the Acts of the Apostles* (London: SCM, 1956), pp. 138-185; Ulrich Wilckens, *Die Missionsreden der Apostelgeschichte,* WMANT 5 (Neukirchen: Neukirchener Verlag, 1963); Paul S. Minear, "Luke's Use of the Birth Stories," in *Studies in Luke-Acts,* ed. Keck and Martyn, pp. 111-130.

11. See Joseph A. Fitzmyer, *The Gospel according to Luke I–IX,* AB (Garden City, N.Y.: Doubleday, 1981), pp. 313-314.

12. Robert C. Tannehill, "Israel in Luke-Acts: A Tragic Story," *JBL* 104 (1985):69-85.

13. See Tiede, *Prophecy and History,* pp. 103-118.

14. See Josephus, *War* 5:362–423, and Melito's "Homily on the Passion."

15. Paul S. Minear, "Dear Theo: The Kerygmatic Intention and Claim of the Book of Acts," *Int* 27 (1973):131-150.

16. See Jervell, "The Circumcised Messiah," trans. Roy A. Harrisville, in *The Unknown Paul,* pp. 138-145.

17. So in Acts 4:11-12, the rejection of Jesus is immediately connected with God's salvation which is available to the "rulers of the people and the elders" only through the name of Jesus.

18. The use of the word "Jew" in Luke-Acts is a conundrum. Its usage in Acts by non-Israelites (18:14; 22:30; 23:27) or by Israelites speaking to non-Israelites (21:39; 23:20; 24:5) fits with the origins of the term in the administration of the region of Judea by the Hellenistic and Roman Empires. In 14:1-2 there are believing and unbelieving Jews, i.e., those who accept the preaching of Paul and Barnabas and those who do not. In 28:17, Paul addresses local Jews, reporting that the Jews in Palestine spoke against him, and they report they have not heard any evil reports from Judea or from the "brothers" who have come. Certainly Zehnle has overstated the case in saying that after Acts 13:43-45 "*hoi Ioudaioi* becomes a *terminus technicus* (as in the Fourth Gospel) for the opponents of Paul, the bringer of salvation" (Richard F. Zehnle, *Peter's*

Pentecost Discourse, SBLMS 15 [Nashville: Abingdon, 1971], p. 65). Here again in Acts 28:24-25, some are persuaded and others disbelieve, and there is division among the Jews.

19. "Book of Jubilees," trans. R. H. Charles, rev. C. Rabin, in *The Apocryphal Old Testament*, ed. H. F. D. Sparks (Oxford: Clarendon, 1984), pp. 11-13.

20. "The Fourth Book of Ezra," trans. Bruce M. Metzger, in *The Old Testament Pseudepigrapha*, vol. 1, ed. James H. Charlesworth (Garden City, N.Y.: Doubleday, 1983), p. 527.

21. "The Syriac Apocalypse of Baruch," trans. R. H. Charles, rev. L. H. Brockington, in *The Apocryphal Old Testament*, ed. Sparks.

22. See Jean Danielou, *The Theology of Jewish Christianity*, trans. John A. Baker (Chicago: Henry Regnery, 1964), p. 165, n. 63: "This is indeed the very definition of Jewish Christian theology." See also John J. Collins, *Between Athens and Jerusalem* (New York: Crossroad, 1983), pp. 154-74.

23. "The Testaments of the Twelve Patriarchs," trans. M. de Jonge, in *The Apocryphal Old Testament*, ed. Sparks, pp. 525, 528. See also the Epistle of Barnabas 14, where the Isaiah passages are cited, but now in the context of Christian displacement of Israel (5:2) as heirs of the covenant.

24. See Tiede, "The Exaltation of Jesus," pp. 285-86.

25. See Jacob Jervell, "The Mighty Minority," in *The Unknown Paul*, pp. 26-51.

Chapter 3. David P. Moessner, "The Ironic Fulfillment of Israel's Glory"

1. David L. Tiede, " 'Glory to Thy People Israel': Luke-Acts and the Jews," above, p. 23.

2. Ibid., pp. 23-29.

3. Ibid., p. 27.

4. Ibid., p. 34.

5. Ibid., p. 24.

6. Robert C. Tannehill, "Israel in Luke-Acts: A Tragic Story," *JBL* 104 (1985): 69-85.

7. Tiede, "Glory to Thy People Israel," p. 25.

8. Cf. Ibid., p. 29.

9. Ibid., p. 28.

10. Ibid., p. 29.

11. Ibid., p. 33.

12. Ibid., p. 28.

13. Ibid., p. 25.

14. Emphasis added.

15. Tiede, "Glory to Thy People Israel," p. 25.

16. Ibid., p. 23.

17. LXX, *parakaleō*, e.g., Isa. 40:1 (twice), 2; 49:13; 51:3, 12, 19.

18. Meir Sternberg, *The Poetics of Biblical Narrative*, Indiana Literary Biblical Series (Bloomington: Indiana University Press, 1985).

19. Ibid., p. 84; cf. Robert Alter, *The Art of Biblical Narrative* (New York: Basic Books, 1981), pp. 155-177.

20. Luke 1:1-4 then would explain to readers unfamiliar with biblical historiography and *consistent* omniscient narration that his work should be compared or aligned with Greco-Roman histories. On the question of genre, see Charles H. Talbert,

NOTES

"Once Again: Gospel Genre," and David P. Moessner, "And Once Again, What Sort of 'Essence'? A Response to Charles Talbert," *Semeia* (1988). Luke appeals to the authority of the *paradosis* of "eyewitnesses and ministers" (1:2) in presenting this omniscient perspective, which is ultimately credited to Jesus himself (e.g., 10:21-24; 24:44-49). As a literary convention, omniscient narration should not be confused or necessarily aligned with philosophical-theological notions of omniscience and biblical authority.
21. I.e., in addition to the "mantle" of "righteous," "pious" Israel (2:25; cf. 1:6; 2:22-24).
22. Cf. the argument in Hebrews 7 with Melchizedek's superiority to Abraham.
23. Cf. Ezek. 14:17.
24. See note 20 above.
25. See Robert C. Tannehill, "Rejection by Jews and Turning to Gentiles: The Pattern of Paul's Mission in Acts," below, chap. 6.
26. Literally "ten thousands," and "many" *(posai)* of them; Acts 4:4 speaks of about 5000 "men."
27. See Jack T. Sanders, "The Jewish People in Luke-Acts," below, chap. 4.
28. See especially David L. Tiede, "The Exaltation of Jesus and the Restoration of Israel in Acts 1," *HTR* 79 (1986): 278-286.
29. David P. Moessner, " 'The Christ Must Suffer': New Light on the Jesus—Peter, Stephen, Paul Parallels in Luke-Acts," *NovT* 28 (1986): 220-56; idem. *Lord of the Banquet: The Literary and Theological Significance of the Lukan Travel Narrative* (Philadelphia: Fortress, 1989).
30. See further David P. Moessner, "Paul in Acts: Preacher of Eschatological Repentance to Israel," *NTS* 34 (1988):96-104.

Chapter 4. Jack T. Sanders, "The Jewish People in Luke-Acts"

1. Jacob Jervell, *Luke and the People of God* (Minneapolis: Augsburg, 1972), p. 44.
2. The phrase is Haenchen's; cf. Ernst Haenchen, "The Book of Acts as Source Material for the History of Early Christianity," in *Studies in Luke-Acts*, ed. Leander E. Keck and J. Louis Martyn (Philadelphia: Fortress, 1966), p. 278.
3. Cf., e.g, Ferdinand Christian Baur, *Paul the Apostle: His Life and Works, His Epistles and Teachings*, ed. Eduard Zeller (London and Edinburgh: Williams and Norgate, 1873) 1:6.
4. W. M. L. DeWette, *Kurze Erklärung der Apostelgeschichte*, 4th ed. rev. Franz Overbeck (Leipzig: Hirzel, 1870); cf. pp. xxx-xxxi.
5. Alfred Loisy, *Les Evangiles synoptiques*, 2 vols. (Ceffonds, près Montier-en-Der [Haute-Marne]: publ. by author, 1907–1908); cf. 2:652; and *Les Actes des Apôtres* (Paris: Nourry, 1920); cf. p. 118.
6. Ernst Haenchen, "Judentum und Christentum in der Apostelgeschichte," *ZNW* 54 (1963):157.
7. Ibid., p. 164.
8. Ibid., pp. 165-66.
9. Ibid., pp. 166-71.
10. Ibid., p. 171.
11. Ibid., p. 173; cf. also idem, *The Acts of the Apostles* (Philadelphia: Westminster, 1971), pp. 414, 417-18.
12. Haenchen, "Judentum und Christentum," p. 175.

143

13. Ibid., pp. 174-75.
14. Ibid., p. 182.
15. Ibid., p. 185.
16. Haenchen, "Source Material," pp. 266, 278.
17. Haenchen, *Acts*, p. 100; emphasis in the original.
18. Adolf Harnack, *The Acts of the Apostles*, New Testament Studies 3 (New York: Putnam's, 1909), cf. p. 287.
19. Hans Conzelmann, *The Theology of St. Luke* (New York: Harper & Brothers, 1960), cf. p. 146; Augustin George, "Israël dans l'oeuvre de Luc," *RB* 75 (1968) 481-525; Jervell, *People of God*, cf. pp. 60-62.
20. Gerhard Lohfink, *Die Sammlung Israels: Eine Untersuchung zur lukanischen Ekklesiologie*, SANT 39 (Munich: Kösel, 1975), p. 30.
21. Ibid., p. 33.
22. Ibid., p. 37.
23. Ibid., pp. 42-43.
24. Ibid., pp. 43-45.
25. Ibid., p. 48.
26. Ibid., p. 54.
27. Ibid., p. 55.
28. Ibid., p. 60.
29. Contra Nils A. Dahl, "A People for His Name," *NTS* 4 (1957–1958): 324-26; idem, "The Story of Abraham in Luke-Acts," in *Studies in Luke-Acts*, p. 151; Harnack, *Acts*, pp. 50-51.
30. Some years ago, when I was a visiting faculty member at a Christian theological school, I asked one of my colleagues there if he really believed the creed that he had earlier that day happily recited as the last requirement for receiving indefinite tenure at that institution. He replied—quite vigorously, I might add—that he believed that the Old Testament had been fulfilled in the New Testament and not in the Talmud. That is Luke's point. As Loisy (*Actes*, p. 830) says, Luke wants to show that Christianity is "the sane interpretation of the most authentic Judaism." Many other authors express the same opinion.
31. Thus also Lohfink, *Sammlung Israels*, p. 60.
32. Samuel Sandmel, *Anti-Semitism in the New Testament?* (Philadelphia: Fortress, 1978), p. 73.
33. Joseph A. Fitzmyer, "Jewish Christianity in Acts in Light of the Qumran Scrolls," in *Studies in Luke-Acts*, pp. 235-236.
34. Cf. the remarks of Walter Eltester, "Israel im lukanischen Werk und die Nazarethperikope," in *Jesus in Nazareth*, ed. Walter Eltester, BZNW 40 (Berlin and New York: Walter de Gruyter, 1972), p. 135.
35. Loisy, *Actes*, pp. 50-121.
36. Stephen is, of course, more important for the development of the narrative in Acts than the space allotted him would indicate, since his martyrdom is the "watershed" (Haenchen) in the geographical progression of the gospel. Also, his importance is greater than might be indicated by the fact that he has only one speech, whereas Jesus, Peter, and Paul speak frequently (cf. Harnack, *Acts*, p. 120). When Stephen did start speaking, he produced the longest speech in Acts, and it was hard to get him to stop.
37. Although some recent authors still maintain that the speech of Stephen is different enough from the other speeches in Acts to warrant considering it as something other than a Lukan composition (cf., e.g., Martin H. Scharlemann,

Stephen: A Singular Saint, AnBib 34 [Rome: Pontifical Biblical Institute, 1968], p. 52), the extensive analysis by M. Sabbe ("The Son of Man Saying in Acts 7, 56," in *Les Actes des Apôtres: Traditions, rédaction, théologie,* ed. J. Kremer, BETL 48 [Gembloux: Editions Duculot; Leuven: University Press, 1979] pp. 251-56), detailing the many correlations between the Stephen episode and the rest of Luke-Acts, renders useless any position that holds that the Stephen episode does not represent Luke's own thinking. Cf. also John J. Kilgallen, *The Stephen Speech: A Literary and Redactional Study of Acts 7, 2-53,* AnBib 67 (Rome: Pontifical Biblical Institute, 1976), esp. p. 121.

38. Emmeram Kränkl, *Jesus der Knecht Gottes: Die heilsgeschichtliche Stellung Jesu in den Reden der Apostelgeschichte,* Biblische Untersuchungen 8, Münchener Universitäts-Schriften, Katholisch-Theologische Fakultät (Regensburg: Pustet, 1972), p. 112, observes that Jewish guilt is a "red thread" in Stephen's speech. (Calling one of Luke's themes a "red thread" is a tradition unto itself in New Testament scholarship.) A number of other authors make the same point; cf. especially Johannes Bihler, *Die Stephanusgeschichte im Zusammenhang der Apostelgeschichte,* Münchener theologische Studien, Historische Abteilung 16 (Munich: Hueber, 1963), pp. 41-81; and Kilgallen, *The Stephen Speech,* pp. 97-104.

39. As, for example, Fridolin Keck proposes in *Die öffentliche Abschiedsrede Jesu in Lk 20, 45-21,36,* Forschung zur Bibel 25 (Stuttgart: Katholisches Bibelwerk, 1976), pp. 198, 321.

40. It is also possible, however, that the prophets are not thought of as being Jews (or Israelites). They may be rather the messengers of God. The same would be true of the apostles and, of course, of Jesus. Jerome H. Neyrey, "Jesus' Address to the Women of Jerusalem (Lk. 23. 27-31)," *NTS* 29 (1983): 76, comes close to this position, as does Luke T. Johnson, *The Literary Function of Possessions in Luke-Acts,* SBLDS 39 (Missoula: Scholars Press, 1977), p. 77.

41. Repetition of language here from 5:30: *kremasantes epi xylou,* cf. the discussion of this point by Kränkl, *Knecht,* pp. 111-112.

42. It is unclear exactly to what *touton* refers. The near antecedent is "the message *(logos)* of this salvation" (13:26), and that may be what Luke intended instead of "him," i.e., the Jerusalem Jews could kill Jesus because they were ignorant of the message of salvation that was contained in the sacred Scripture that they heard weekly.

43. This is correctly seen by a few authors but is widely misunderstood. Johannes Bihler, "Der Stephanusbericht (Apg 6,8-15 und 7,54-8,2)," *BZ* N.F. 3 (1959): 266, n. 40, emphasizes that Stephen's speech contains no "call for repentance"; and he astutely observes that the ignorance theme of Luke 23:34 is missing from its parallel in Acts 7:60 *(Stephanusgeschichte,* p. 18).

44. Cf. Conzelmann, *Theology,* p. 90: "After the resurrection . . . unbelief becomes inexcusable."

45. It was Martin Dibelius who first pointed out that the three announcements— here, in 18:6, and in 28:28—occur, geographically significantly, in Asia Minor, on the Greek mainland, and in Rome. Cf. Martin Dibelius, *Studies in the Acts of the Apostles,* ed. Heinrich Greeven (New York: Scribner's, 1956), p. 150. Haenchen's point *(Acts,* pp. 414, 417-18) that the rejection of the Antiochene Jews has implications for worldwide Jewry is therefore surely justified. Stephen G. Wilson, *The Gentiles and the Gentile Mission in Luke-Acts,* SNTSMS 23

(Cambridge: At the University Press, 1973), p. 223, correctly claims that Jervell misinterprets Acts 13:46 when he makes it support his contention that it was Jewish acceptance, not rejection of the gospel that led to the Gentile mission. Jervell repeats the position in *The Unknown Paul* (Minneapolis: Augsburg, 1984), pp. 16, 133.

46. Thus Joachim Gnilka, *Die Verstockung Israels: Isaias 6, 9-10 in der Theologie der Synoptiker,* SANT 3 (Munich: Kösel, 1961), p. 148, points out that the Jewish response to Paul's mission should have been no surprise, since "it finds its ultimate foundation in the logic of Israel's history."

47. So correctly Robert Maddox, *The Purpose of Luke-Acts,* FRLANT 126 (Göttingen: Vandenhoeck & Ruprecht, 1982), pp. 43-44. Maddox further finds a "progressive intensification" in Paul's three announcements of rejecting the Jews: "At the end of Paul's mission the opportunity offered [to the Jews] at its beginning has been lost" (ibid.).

48. Haenchen, "Source Material," p. 278; cf. further idem, *Acts,* p. 693.

49. Ulrich Wilckens, *Die Missionsreden der Apostelgeschichte,* 3rd ed., WMANT 5 (Neukirchen-Vluyn: Neukirchener Verlag, 1974), pp. 178-186.

50. Emphasized also by Bihler, *Stephanusgeschichte,* pp. 81, 92.

51. This realization, it seems to me, also reveals the mistake of the argument of David L. Tiede, *Prophecy and History in Luke-Acts* (Philadelphia: Fortress, 1980), p. 81, that the judgment sayings against Jerusalem in the Gospel "derive from *within* the Jewish scriptural heritage" (emphasis his), thus placing Luke within the prophetic tradition. That the Lukan Peter accuses the Jews to Cornelius, however, explodes the notion that Luke belongs within the prophetic tradition (whatever the source[s] of his accusatory language). For Luke, the Jews are "other."

52. Cf. J. C. O'Neill, *The Theology of Acts in Its Historical Setting,* 2nd ed. (London: SPCK, 1970), p. 84: "Luke's primary theological interest . . . is to show how the Jews rejected each opportunity to repent."

53. It will not do to observe that Stephen's speech contains no such call to repentance because he was cut short. Such an explanation takes a too naively historical approach. Stephen's speech was cut short, not by the Sanhedrin nor by the Jewish mob, but by Luke, who thus saw to it that Stephen offered no call to repentance.

54. Malcolm Tolbert, "Leading Ideas of the Gospel of Luke," *RevExp* 64 (1967): 442.

55. Most commentators find a comparison in the narrative rather than a contrast, i.e., that Jesus' saying means that, whereas there is faith—even great faith—among Jews, this Gentile faith is even greater. The text, however, presents a contrast.

56. Cf. further the thorough discussion by Joseph A. Fitzmyer, *The Gospel According to Luke,* 2 vols., AB (Garden City, N. Y.: Doubleday, 1981–1985), 1:679, who agrees that "this generation" is "the Palestinian contemporaries of John and Jesus."

57. The different parts of the Lukan saying do not appear together in Matthew.

58. The parables of the good Samaritan, of the prodigal son, and of the Pharisee and the toll collector have primary relevance in discussions of outcasts and of the Pharisees in Luke-Acts and are omitted here.

59. Cf. also Sandmel, *Anti-Semitism?* pp. 78-80.

60. Cf. the discussion of this point in Robert W. Funk, *Language, Hermeneutic, and Word of God* (New York: Harper and Row, 1966), pp. 164-167, 172-175.

NOTES

61. Thus Gerhard Schneider, *Das Evangelium nach Lukas,* Ökumenischer Taschenbuchkommentar zum Neuen Testament (Gütersloh: Mohn; Würzburg: Echter Verlag, 1977), 2:318, correctly connects this saying of the Lukan Jesus to Paul's concluding denunciation at the end of Acts. The argument of Eric Franklin, *Christ the Lord* (Philadelphia: Westminster, 1975), p. 142, that the rejection is only of "those who refused the original invitation," not of "the Jewish nation as a whole," robs the parable of its most obvious point.

62. Here, as with all the parables, most authors are primarily interested in the original parable, not in what Luke makes of it. Loisy, *Evangiles synoptiques,* 2:177-178, Erich Klostermann, *Das Lukasevangelium,* HNT, 2nd ed. (Tübingen: Mohr [Siebeck], 1929), p. 170, and C. G. Montefiore, *The Synoptic Gospels,* 2nd ed. (London: Macmillan, 1927), 2:540, however, see that the present parable is understandable only in terms of the Christian belief in Jesus' resurrection. Loisy's comment is on the mark: The "five brothers, who have Moses and the Prophets at hand, represent Judaism; they do not know how to find Christ there. . . . Thus the parable becomes an allegory that explains the reprobation of the Jews. . . . The rich man of the primitive parable has therefore been taken, himself, as a first type of the Jewish incredulity and Lazarus as the type of the Jewish Christian, which they weren't originally" *(Evangiles synoptiques,* 2:177).

63. Cf. esp. Adolf Jülicher, *Die Gleichnisreden Jesu,* reprint ed. (Darmstadt: Wissenschaftliche Buchgesellschaft, 1963), pp. 472-495; and my article, "The Parable of the Pounds and Lucan Anti-Semitism," *TS* 42 (1981): 660-668, where other modern literature is also cited.

64. Josef Ernst, *Das Evangelium nach Lukas,* RNT (Regensburg: Pustet, 1977), pp. 519, 521, seems to have seen the point exactly: Luke 19:14 means that "Judaism rejects the Messiah Jesus"; and the relation of the destruction of Jerusalem in the year 70 to the slaughter of the opponents in 19:27 is that of an example.

65. This is the approach taken by Loisy, *Evangiles synoptiques,* 2:253, who argues that the two tax collectors, Zacchaeus and Levi (5:29), are types of pagan converts. Cf. further Julius Wellhausen, *Das Evangelium Lucae* (Berlin: Georg Reimer, 1904), p. 104: Zacchaeus is a *"Doppelgänger* of Levi." Fitzmyer, *Luke,* 2:1221, denies any connection with Gal. 3:7.

66. While the manuscript evidence for the originality of this verse is weak, it must surely be original, since it and the saying in v. 46 about entrusting himself to God's care are the prototypes for Stephen's last words in Acts 7:59-60.

67. So Alfred Loisy, *L'Evangile selon Luc* (Paris: Nourry, 1942), p. 556, Kränkl, *Knecht,* p. l06, and Walter Grundmann, *Das Evangelium nach Lukas,* THKNT, 7th ed. (Berlin: Evangelische Verlagsanstalt, 1974), pp. 432-433.

68. Cf. above, pp. 53-54.

69. For example, Luke 3:21; 19:48; 24:19; Acts 2:47; 3:11; 13:24. The situation is similar with the "crowd" or "crowds"; cf. Luke 6:19, "All the crowd sought to touch him." Lohfink, *Sammlung Israels,* pp. 43-46, sees especially the problems that the contrast between speech and narrative creates in 4:16-30, but he remains convinced that the one is source and the other "redaction"; but such an explanation is insufficient to explain the present form of the Gospel. To write that "Luke certainly saw, but took into account" the tension thus created in the Nazareth pericope (ibid., p. 46) is also no further help.

70. Unfortunately successful, one must add.

71. Cf. the discussion in Walter Radl, *Paulus und Jesus im lukanischen Doppel-werk: Untersuchungen zu Parallelmotiven im Lukasevangelium und in der Apos-telgeschichte,* Europäische Hochschulschriften (Bern: Herbert Lang; Frankfurt am Main: Peter Lang, 1975), pp. 299-301; the phrase, *"auf Jesu Seite [ste-hend],"* occurs on p. 302. Cf. also Lohfink, *Sammlung Israels,* p. 37.

72. Cf. also Conzelmann, *Theology,* p. 87.

73. The well-known proposal of Gottfried Rau, "Das Volk in der lukanischen Passionsgeschichte: Eine Konjektur zu Lk 23:13," *ZNW* 56 (1965): 41-51, esp. pp. 43, 48-50, that one should take as original a variant reading of Luke 23:13, "... the rulers *of* the people," must be rejected in view of v. 4, which already brings the "crowds" (= "people") into collusion with the priests. Cf. Lohfink, *Sammlung Israels,* pp. 37, 43, and Schneider, *Lukas,* 2:477. Radl's phrase (*Paulus und Jesus,* p. 295) is apt: The people are the "loud volume gallery at the trial."

74. Gerhard Schneider, *Verleugnung, Verspottung und Verhör Jesu nach Lukas 22, 54-71,* SANT 22 (Munich: Kösel, 1969), p. 193, takes the action to indicate remorse. Gerhard Lohfink, "Hat Jesus eine Kirche gestiftet?" *TQ* 161 (1981):88, sees in it attestation for his claim that Luke "represents the relation of people to Jesus more positively than [does] Mark." Fitzmyer, *Luke,* 2:1476, sees that "the 'crowds' are here associated with the authorities," but he argues that this does not mean that the people concur in the accusation.

75. Joachim Wanke, *Die Emmauserzählung: Eine redaktionsgeschichtliche Unter-suchung zu Lk 24, 13-35,* Erfurter theologische Studien 31 (Leipzig: St. Benno, 1973), p. 66, suggests that the primary motif in the disciples' statement of disappointment is that Jesus, having been killed, could not be the Messiah, as they had hoped.

76. Since "apostles" is the near antecedent, it might look as if Luke meant that the two were apostles, but this could hardly be the case, since Luke in 6:13 had designated the Twelve as apostles, whereas the one on the Emmaus road who is named Cleopas is not one of the Twelve. Luke probably means "of them" in a more general sense, i.e., one of those who were among the followers of Jesus and vitally concerned with his death.

77. On the topic of parallel structure, cf. especially Radl, *Paulus und Jesus,* and Charles H. Talbert, *Literary Patterns, Theological Themes, and the Genre of Luke-Acts,* SBLMS 20 (Missoula: Scholars Press, 1974).

78. Also Conzelmann, *Theology,* p. 145 n. 2.

79. On this point cf. especially Christoph Burchard, *Der dreizehnte Zeuge: Tra-ditions- und kompositionsgeschichtliche Untersuchungen zu Lukas' Darstellung der Frühzeit des Paulus,* FRLANT 103 (Göttingen: Vandenhoeck & Ruprecht, 1970), p. 113.

80. E.g., Jervell, *People of God,* pp. 41-74; Franklin, *Christ the Lord,* pp. 77-115.

81. His opponents are called only "some" in 19:9, but, since they are in the synagogue and oppose "the way," they can only be Jews.

82. How little this "simulacrum of history" (Loisy) is based on any real information about past events is seen in the summary narrative of Acts 14:21b-28. Here Paul goes back over territory where he had earlier experienced such occasionally vigorous opposition from Jews, continuing his preaching (v. 25), and there is not a breath of Jewish hostility anywhere.

83. On the appropriateness of this term, cf. Radl, *Paulus und Jesus,* pp. 68-267.

The point is also very well made by Joseph B. Tyson, "The Jewish Public in Luke-Acts," *NTS* 30 (1984):582.

84. Cf. the remark of Jacques Dupont, "La conclusion des Actes et son rapport à l'ensemble de l'ouvrage de Luc," in *Les Actes des Apôtres,* p. 401, that "Nazareth, Antioch of Pisidia, Rome [are] three landmarks of the same history, three situations permitting variations on the same theme."

85. Many authors have noted that Luke 4:16-30, with its summary judgment on the Jews, is "programmatic" for Luke-Acts; cf., e.g., Fitzmyer, *Luke,* 1:526-29.

86. On this point, Jervell, *People of God,* p. 64, is more correct than all those who emphasize that the individual Jew can always convert, when he writes that "Luke has excluded the possibility of a further mission to Jews for the Church of his time because the judgment by and on the Jews has been irrevocably passed."

87. Lohfink, *Sammlung Israels,* pp. 42-43, has seen this but has misunderstood it, inasmuch as he thinks that the general Jewish guilt demonstrated in Luke 23 prepares the way for later Jewish repentance.

88. The words are those of Tolbert, "Leading Ideas," p. 445, but the sentiment is repeated by many other authors.

89. This realization should allow us to lay to rest those explanations, such as that of Gnilka, *Verstockung,* p. 151, of the role of the Jews in Luke-Acts that capitalize on the distinction between leaders and people and thus make Luke appear less anti-Semitic than he is. Gnilka even goes so far as to say that the way in which Luke uses the distinction avoids "wounding . . . Jews" (ibid.). Whether he asked any Jew to read Luke-Acts and to corroborate that opinion he does not say. But to reiterate: the distinction does not occur in the *speeches* of Jesus, Peter, Stephen, and Paul, and it disappears in the *narrative* in the Pauline passion.

90. Cf. O'Neill, *Theology,* p. 87: Paul's concluding remarks in Acts sum "up the verdict of God on all the Jews, a verdict painfully discovered by the Church throughout the whole of Acts."

91. Robert C. Tannehill, "The Mission of Jesus according to Luke IV 16-30," in *Jesus in Nazareth,* p. 60 (emphasis added). Cf. also Tyson, "Jewish Public," p. 578.

92. Robert C. Tannehill, "Israel in Luke-Acts: A Tragic Story," *JBL* 104 (1985): 75.

93. Ibid., p. 74 (emphasis added).

94. The degrees to which one may speak of the Gospel of Luke, and Acts too, as tragedies has now been thoroughly and adequately discussed by Joseph B. Tyson, *The Death of Jesus in Luke-Acts* (Columbia: University of South Carolina Press, 1986), pp. 12-16, 35-38.

Chapter 5. Marilyn Salmon, "Insider or Outsider? Luke's Relationship with Judaism"

1. Jack T. Sanders, "The Jewish People in Luke-Acts," above, p. 58.

2. David L. Tiede, " 'Glory to Thy People Israel': Luke-Acts and the Jews," above, p. 25.

3. Sanders, "The Jewish People," p. 59.

4. Ibid., p. 71.

5. Sanders and I are in agreement that Luke distinguishes between believing and nonbelieving Pharisees. We differ in our assessment of his motive. See Jack T. Sanders, "The Pharisees in Luke-Acts," in *The Living Text: Essays in Honor of Ernest W. Saunders*, ed. Dennis Groh and Robert Jewett (New York: University Press of America, 1985), pp. 141-188.

6. See Jacob Jervell, "The Law in Luke-Acts," in *Luke and the People of God* (Minneapolis: Augsburg, 1972), p. 140.

7. See, for example, Acts 21:22-26; 23:4-5.

8. The circumcision of Timothy, whose mother was a believing Jew, follows the apostolic decree in which Gentiles, though exempt from circumcision, are instructed to observe dietary and chastity laws. I think the juxtaposition of these is significant.

9. See Jervell, "The Law," for an extensive treatment of this issue.

10. See Josephus, *War* 11:162-163; *Life* 11.

11. Sanders, "The Jewish People," p. 73.

12. Ibid.

Chapter 6. Robert C. Tannehill, "Rejection by Jews and Turning to Gentiles: The Pattern of Paul's Mission in Acts"

1. Comments on other aspects of the Lukan attitude toward the Jews may be found in a previous article See Robert C. Tannehill, "Israel in Luke-Acts: A Tragic Story," *JBL* 104 (1985):69-85. The present essay, which is a revised version of a paper previously published in *SBL Seminar Papers*, ed. Kent Harold Richards (Atlanta: Scholars Press, 1986), pp. 130-141, provides further support for the position broadly sketched in the previous article.

2. See Ulrich Wilckens, *Die Missionsreden der Apostelgeschichte*, 3rd ed., WMANT 5 (Neukirchen-Vluyn: Neukirchener Verlag, 1974), p. 53.

3. Acts 13:23,32,33a formulate the *Leitgedanken* of the speech, as indicated by Matthäus Franz-Josef Buss, *Die Missionspredigt des Apostels Paulus im Pisidischen Antiochien* (Stuttgart: Katholisches Bibelwerk, 1980), p. 29.

4. The association of Jesus' role as "Savior" with his role as Davidic Messiah is typical of Luke-Acts. See Luke 1:69; 2:11.

5. Variant reading: "to you."

6. The narrator distinguishes between the resurrection and exaltation of Jesus in Acts 1 in order to emphasize Jesus' careful instruction of the apostles. However, when Jesus' messianic enthronement is the main concern, this distinction can be ignored.

7. For further argument supporting the view that 13:33 refers to Jesus' resurrection, see Evald Lövestam, *Son and Saviour: A Study of Acts 13, 32-37* (Lund: C. W. K. Gleerup, 1961), pp. 8-10; Emmeram Kränkl, *Jesus der Knecht Gottes: Die heilsgeschichtliche Stellung Jesu in den Reden der Apostelgeschichte*, Biblische Untersuchungen 8, Münchener Universitäts-Schriften, Katholisch Theologische Fakultät (Regensburg: Pustet, 1972), pp. 137-138; and Robert F. O'Toole, "Christ's Resurrection in Acts 13, 13-52," *Bib* 60 (1979): 361-372.

8. Marcel Dumais compares the scriptural interpretation in the speech to Jewish midrash, arguing that the methods of interpretation as well as the themes are appropriate to the Jewish synagogue. See *Le langage de l'évangélisation: L'annonce missionnaire en milieu juif (Actes 13, 16-41)* (Tournai: Desclée & Montréal: Bellarmin, 1976).

9. See Hans Conzelmann, *Die Apostelgeschichte*, HNT 7 (Tubingen: J. C. B. Mohr, 1963), p. 77: "*ta pista* wird als 'unvergänglich' aufgefasst." E. Lövestam detects a double aspect to the promise in 13:34: "The covenant promise to David had . . . a *firm* and *irrevocable* nature. This promise similarly concerned *permanent* dominion." See *Son and Saviour*, p. 79 (emphasis in the original).

10. M. Buss emphasizes the close terminological and thematic connection of the Antioch speech with Luke 1–2; see *Die Missionspredigt*, p. 146.

11. Walter Bauer interprets *ta hosia* as divine decrees, in contrast to human ones. See *A Greek-English Lexicon of the New Testament and Other Early Christian Literature*, translated and adapted by W. F. Arndt and F. W. Gingrich (Chicago: University of Chicago Press, 1957) s.v. Jacques Dupont objects to this. He says that use of the phrase to mean religious duties, in contrast to social duties, is well established, but the meaning "divine decrees" is doubtful. See "TA ΟΣΙΑ ΔΑΥΙΔ ΠΙΣΤΑ (Ac XIII 34 = Is LV3)," *RB* 68 (1961) 95. Dupont's criticism leads me to suggest that the narrator may have understood *ta hosia* to refer to the religious duties of David as king and therefore to what we would call the "office" of king. This royal office will be established for the Jewish people through the coming of their Messiah, according to 13:34.

12. See Ernst Haenchen, *The Acts of the Apostles* (Philadelphia: Westminster, 1971), p. 729.

13. In Acts 20:26-27 Paul declares that he is "clean from the blood of all" because of his dedicated preaching.

14. It is interesting that Paul is presented here as directly denying anti-Judaism on his part. While this does not settle the modern question of whether the Paul of Acts is anti-Jewish, it at least lets us know how the narrator wishes to present Paul.

15. See Paul Schubert, "The Final Cycle of Speeches in the Book of Acts," *JBL* 87 (1968):1-16.

16. See Klaus Haacker, "Das Bekenntnis des Paulus zur Hoffnung Israels nach der Apostelgeschichte des Lukas," *NTS* 31 (1985): 437-451. Haacker's interpretation, developed as a critique of Haenchen, is in many ways congenial with the interpretation I am about to offer. Haacker rightly places Paul's loyalty to the hope of Israel in the broader context of the Lukan emphasis on the fulfillment of Israel's hope, an emphasis that begins with the birth narrative (Luke 1–2). On the significance of the birth narrative for our theme, see Robert C. Tannehill, *The Narrative Unity of Luke-Acts* (Philadelphia: Fortress, 1986), 1:15-44.

17. On the Messiah's kingdom as an eternal kingdom, recall the preceding discussion of Luke 1:32-33; Acts 13:34.

18. The significance of both the broad contours of the story and of details of its presentation become clearer when we recognize the tragic aspect of Israel's story in Luke-Acts. See R. Tannehill, "Israel in Luke-Acts," pp. 69-85.

19. This is the conclusion of Hermann J. Hauser, *Strukturen der Abschlusserzählung der Apostelgeschichte (Apg 28, 16-31)*, AnBib 86 (Rome: Pontifical Biblical Institute, 1979), pp. 64-66.

20. Paul is portrayed as a prophet on the model of the scriptural prophets through applying Septuagintal language from prophetic calls to him. See Acts 18:6 (cf. Ezek. 33:4); 18:9-10 (cf. Jer. 1:7-8); 26:16-18 (cf. Ezek. 2:1,3; Jer. 1:7-8; Isa. 42:6-7). In speaking the harsh words in Acts 28:26-27, Paul is fulfilling a prophetic role well-established in Israel's Scripture, where prophetic indictments of the people are common.

21. These words are addressed to the prophet, not to the people, and it would not have been necessary to include them in the quotation. However, their inclusion emphasizes the divine command behind the prophetic role which Paul is fulfilling at this point in the story.

22. Part of the preceding paragraph is adapted from my article, "Israel in Luke-Acts," p. 83.

23. These passages are noted by H. Hauser, *Abschlusserzählung,* p. 109.

24. See Francis Pereira, *Ephesus: Climax of Universalism in Luke-Acts: A Redaction-Critical Study of Paul's Ephesian Ministry (Acts 18:23—20:1)* (Anand, India: Gujarat Sahitya Prakash, 1983). Pereira emphasizes that Paul's lengthy mission in Ephesus is, according to Acts, a universal mission, directed at the same time to Jews and Gentiles.

25. See, e.g., H. Hauser, *Abschlusserzählung,* p. 118.

26. Jacques Dupont, in "La conclusion des Actes et son rapport à l'ensemble de l'ouvrage de Luc," in *Nouvelles études sur les Actes des Apôtres* (Paris: Éditions du Cerf, 1984), discusses the relation of the end of Acts to Paul's sermon in the Antioch synagogue. He remarks (p. 487), "Le long discours de 13, 16-39 donne une idée de ce que Luc peut avoir dans la tête quand, en 28,23, il résume en deux mots le contenu d'une prédication qui a duré 'depuis le matin jusqu'au soir.' " I would add that Paul is still repeating the same message in 28:31.

Chapter 7. Michael J. Cook, "The Mission to the Jews in Acts: Unraveling Luke's 'Myth of the "Myriads" ' "

1. Quoted from Samuel Sandmel, *Anti-Semitism in the New Testament?* (Philadelphia: Fortress, 1978), p. 100.

2. E.g., in Iconium (Acts 14:2-6; cf. Lystra [14:19]); Thessalonica (17:5; cf. Beroea [17:10-13]); Corinth (18:4-6, 12-13); Ephesus (19:8-9); Jerusalem (21:27-28).

3. Acts 21:20 summarizes "myriads," so termed in the Greek. In English, "myriads" denotes "tens of thousands," but Acts 21:20 seems to refer to "thousands" only; cf. B. H. Throckmorton Jr., "Myriad," *IDB* (1962), 3:478. Even so, many scholars use "myriads" to refer to the new Jewish believers in Acts. Jacob Jervell, *Luke and the People of God* (Minneapolis: Augsburg, 1972), p. 44, lists the key passages: "Mass conversions of Jews are again and again reported: 2:41 [about 3000] (47) [others added day by day]; 4:4 [about 5000 men and, possibly, additional women]; 5:14 [more than ever were added, multitudes]; 6:1 [disciples were increasing], 7 [multiplied greatly]; 9:42; 12:24; 13:43; 14:1; 17:10ff.; (19:20); 21:20 [many myriads]." He understands the "myriads" as literally "tens of thousands" (pp. 45-46).

4. This assessment underlies 2 Cor. 3:14 ("[the Israelites'] minds were hardened"; cf. Michael J. Cook, "The Ties that Blind: II Cor. 3:12ff.," in *When Jews and Christians Meet,* ed. Jakob Petuchowski [Albany: State University of New York Press, 1988]). Also Rom. 9:30-33 (resisting Christ, they have not attained righteousness); 10:1-4 ("not enlightened"); 10:16-19 ("have not all heeded the gospel"); 10:21 (a "contrary people"); 11:7 ("hardened," in a "stupor," they neither "see" nor "hear . . . down to this very day"); 11:11-15 (their "trespass," "failure," "rejection"); 11:20 ("[branches] . . . broken off because of . . . unbelief"); 11:25 (the "hardening" of most [cf. "the rest," 11:7] of Israel).

5. E.g., David L. Tiede, *Prophecy and History in Luke-Acts* (Philadelphia: Fortress, 1980), p. 10.

6. See Tannehill, "Rejection by Jews and Turning to Gentiles: The Pattern of Paul's Mission in Acts," above, chap. 6.
7. As Tannehill has written elsewhere as well: "Israel in Luke-Acts: A Tragic Story," *JBL* 104 (1985): 69-85.
8. Cf. Norman A. Beck, *Mature Christianity* (Selinsgrove, Pa.: Susquehanna University Press, 1985), p. 230: "The Lukan playwright may have been as sophisticated as Jervell supposes, but the same level of sophistication can hardly be attributed to the audience of the literary drama."
9. "The author . . . writes not for a learned public . . . but . . . for a more or less nonliterary congregation"; cf. Ernst Haenchen, "The Book of Acts as Source Material for the History of Early Christianity," in *Studies in Luke-Acts*, ed. Leander E. Keck and J. Louis Martyn (Philadelphia: Fortress, 1980), p. 260.
10. In this chapter all indications of emphasis (italics) in biblical quotations have been added.
11. Joseph B. Tyson, "The Jewish Public in Luke-Acts," *NTS* 30 (1984): 582.
12. Cf. Vernon K. Robbins, "By Land and By Sea: The We-Passages and Ancient Sea Voyages," in *Perspectives on Luke-Acts*, ed. C. H. Talbert (Danville, Va.: Assoc. of Baptist Professors of Religion, 1978), pp. 215-242, esp. 229ff. His concern is with the "we-passages," not with the issues Tannehill raises.
13. "Jewish Public."
14. That Tyson discovers the pattern to pervade both Lukan volumes confirms how fundamental this motif is for Luke.
15. Robbins might agree that his study bears relevance to issues raised by Tannehill; I am not suggesting he would necessarily agree.
16. Tyson, "Jewish Public," p. 581; emphasis added. I am applying Tyson's observation to the problem of whether Luke urges a continued mission to Jews. While this is not a direct concern of his essay, his observations will have a bearing on this discussion.
17. Ibid., 582; emphasis added.
18. Ibid., 581; emphasis added.
19. Luke 2:21ff.; "to do for him according to the custom of the law" (2:27).
20. Luke 4:15ff.; 4:16 is Luke's only use of "their" with "synagogue(s)".
21. Cf. Jack T. Sanders, *The Jews in Luke-Acts* (Philadelphia: Fortress, 1987), p. 33: "Luke makes . . . [these] points for his Gentile readership: . . . that Christianity has not broken with . . . ancient Israelite religion, . . . that . . . continuity runs from Moses and the Prophets to the church; and . . . that it is not Christianity that has rejected Judaism, but Judaism . . . Christianity." I would say "but *Jews* . . . Christianity"; cf. Sandmel, *Anti-Semitism*, p. 77.
22. Gamaliel is unmentioned in the Epistles. Morton S. Enslin notes disparities between Paulinism and traditions ascribable to Gamaliel and later Rabbinic Judaism. Cf. his "Paul and Gamaliel," *JR* 7 (1927): 360-75.
23. Acts 16:3. Luke would have us believe that Timothy, as the son of a Jewish mother, was to be considered a Jew; hence the assent of Paul (himself Jewish) to circumcise him would not have been inconsistent with Paul's rejection of this rite for Gentiles. Yet the real Paul opposed (new) circumcision on principle (cf. Gal. 5:2-12; 1 Cor. 7:18f.). Cf. Philipp Vielhauer, "On the 'Paulinism' of Acts," in Keck and Martyn, *Studies*, p. 40: "Circumcision is [an] . . . acknowledgment of the saving significance of the law, a denial of baptism, . . . [it] splits the church. . . . The circumcision of Timothy stands in direct contradiction to the theology of Paul."

24. An episode related so briefly (Acts 18:18) that Luke's intent can be scarcely other than demonstrating Paul's fidelity to the Law.
25. Acts 21:20ff. Cf. Sandmel, *Anti-Semitism*, p. 94: "How remote this is from . . . Galatians and Romans, where Paul portrays the Law as . . . nullified. How compliantly Paul, who has there spoken against the Law, here observed it!"
26. "The charge . . . [that Paul was teaching] apostasy from Moses was entirely appropriate. . . . Had Paul followed the advice of James . . . he would have been . . . denying his . . . gospel. . . . It is . . . difficult to assume that James, who knew Paul['s] . . . gospel and mission, could have suggested such a deception" (Vielhauer, "Paulinism," pp. 39-40).
27. Acts 23:6; cf. 24:21. See Stephen G. Wilson, *The Gentiles and the Gentile Mission in Luke-Acts*, SNTSMS 23 (Cambridge: At the University Press, 1973), pp. 253-55.
28. Cf. Mark 16:7; Matt. 28:7, 10, 16ff.
29. Luke 24:13ff.; note the designation of Jerusalem as a "Kontinuitätssymbol" by Gerhard Lohfink, *Die Sammlung Israels: Eine Untersuchung zur lukanische Ekklesiologie*, SANT 39 (Munich: Kösel-Verlag, 1975), p. 46; cf. Sanders, *Jews*, pp. 33, 349, notes 67-68.
30. While Matt. 26:56 essentially retains Mark 14:50, Luke omits the Markan passage (see 22:53).
31. Luke 24:47,52; Acts 1:8, 12ff.; cf. Howard Teeple, "The Historical Beginnings of the Resurrection Faith," in *Studies in New Testament and Early Christian Literature: Essays in Honor of Allen P. Wikgren*, ed. David Aune, NovTSup 33 (Leiden: E. J. Brill, 1972), p. 111: "Luke suppresses [the disciples' flight] by omitting the Marcan statements and by creating the fiction that the disciples remained in Jerusalem after the crucifixion."
32. Luke 24:6 transforms predictions of appearances in Galilee (Mark 16:7; Matt. 28:7) into the recollection that Jesus, while previously in Galilee, had revealed his impending death and resurrection (to occur, as it turned out, in the area of Jerusalem).
33. E.g., "Daughters of Jerusalem," Luke 23:28.
34. Luke 2:4ff.; cf. Teeple, "Historical Beginnings," p. 109; Raymond E. Brown, *The Birth of the Messiah: A Commentary on the Infancy Narratives in Matthew and Luke* (Garden City, N.Y.: Doubleday, 1979), pp. 412ff.; Appendices 3 and 7.
35. Luke 2:41ff.; cf. Brown, *Birth*, pp. 485ff.
36. Cf. Samuel Sandmel, "Herod," *IDB* (1962), 2:593. Herod Antipas's presence (cf. Luke 23:15) enables Luke to bring to six the opinions, in chapter 23, that Jesus was innocent (cf. 23:4, 14, 22, 41, 47).
37. Enslin views the itineraries as crafted by Luke in reliance upon Paul's Epistles; cf. Morton S. Enslin, " 'Luke' and Paul," *JAOS* 58 (1938): 81ff.; idem, "Once Again, Luke and Paul," *ZNW* 61 (1970): 253-271.
38. Though precisely how is unclear; cf. Gal. 1:13,23; 1 Cor. 15:9; Phil. 3:6.
39. Sanders, *Jews*, p. 287, terms "preposterous" the notion that Jerusalem priests had authority to arrest heretics in Syria (cf. Acts 9:1-2; 22:4-5).
40. Luke 22:67-70 (cf. Mark 14:55-61a; Matt. 26:59-63a). Some suggest that Luke deferred this accusation until Acts 6:13, where, in any event, the audience notes that the accusation was lodged by false witnesses bent on "stir[ring] up the people" (Acts 6:12). The impression of Jesus' loyalty to the temple is thus preserved unimpaired.

41. In Luke 22:71, he neither tears his mantle nor pronounces Jesus blasphemous (cf. Mark 14:63). The "high priest" (Mark 14:60-61) becomes "they" also in Luke 22:66,70. While Mark 14:53 has Jesus "led . . . to the high priest," Luke 22:54 reads "the high priest's house" (thereby rendering the air of interrogation less official).

42. Luke 22:63f. In Mark, the mocking (14:65) follows the Sanhedrin pericope (14:55-64); so also in Matthew (26:67-68, after 26:59-66).

43. Respecting *false* charges, when Paul is accused of attempting to "profane the temple" (Acts 24:6), a denial is immediately proffered (24:12). The evil intent of the *Jews* is what is inferred, not wrongdoing by Paul. Elsewhere, Luke informs us of "Jews . . . bringing against him many serious charges which they could not prove" (25:7). The Lukan Paul's willingness to circumcise Timothy (16:3) exposes, for the audience, the falsity of the later accusation that Paul tells "Jews . . . among the Gentiles . . . not to circumcise their children" (21:21). Similar is the charge that Jesus forbade payment of tribute to Caesar (Luke 23:2), when the audience already knows (from 20:25) the allegation to be false.

44. Acts 5:34ff. Cf. Sanders, *Jews*, p. 243: "That the Pharisees are 'the very best party' [cf. 26:5] in Judaism . . . has to do with . . . their support of the apostles and of Paul in their trials. By this tactic Luke highlights the point that Christianity is related to Judaism, . . . the authentic continuation. . . ."

45. "Scribes of the Pharisees' party" was Luke's own construction, based on Mark 2:16 ("scribes *of* the Pharisees"; cf. Mark 7:1,5) and Mark 12:28 (the scribe affirming Jesus on "resurrection"). In recounting Paul's trial, Luke introduced "scribes" since he had both learned of their opposition to Sadducees (Mark 12:28), and also wanted to conform Paul to Jesus, who was tried by a Sanhedrin containing scribes (Mark 14:53; 15:1). Formulating one group opposing Sadducees ("scribes *of* the Pharisees' party"; cf. Mark 2:16) was preferable to a more unwieldy "scribes and Pharisees." These four passages (Acts 23:9, Mark 2:16; 7:1,5) have generated erroneous notions: that "scribes" were a Pharisee subgroup; and that Sadducees, too, had *their* "scribes" (inferred from "scribes of the Pharisees' party"). But "scribes," in Mark 2:16; 7:1,5, are editorial retrojections, intended to show that Jerusalem-based scribes, present in pre-Markan passion traditions, were also active earlier in the plot, in Jesus' Galilean ministry. Cf. Michael J. Cook, *Mark's Treatment of the Jewish Leaders*, NovTSup 51 (Leiden: E. J. Brill, 1978), pp. 17ff., 26ff., 63-67, 71-76, 88-97. Acts 23:9, drawing on these passages, is not therefore a reliable basis for determining the relation of "scribes" to Pharisees, let alone to Sadducees.

46. Acts 25:8. "Acts portrays the Gentile missionary Paul as . . . utterly loyal to the law . . . as if . . . the Apostle had never said anything affecting Judaism in the very least" (Vielhauer, "Paulinism," pp. 38, 40).

47. Scholars inclined to view Luke himself as a Jewish Christian may rely on the very examples detailed above—illustrations of fidelity to Judaism by Lukan heroes. To do so is fundamentally to misread Luke's intent. He applies these motifs to demonstrate that Christianity is the continuation of authentic Judaism. In no way should they suggest that Luke himself was a Jewish Christian.

48. Cf., e.g., Acts 11:1-18; 15:1-29; 21:20. "If Luke knows of *Jewish* opposition to *Christianity*, he also knows of Jewish-*Christian* opposition to *Gentile* Christianity" (Sanders, *Jews*, p. 315; emphasis his); "[Luke] comes to the opinion that all Jews are equally, in principle at least, perverse; and he turns his attack

on all together, without distinction" (ibid., p. 317; cf. pp. 284, 304ff. [citing Overbeck], 315ff. [citing Trocmé]).
49. Cf. Robert L. Maddox, *The Purpose of Luke-Acts,* FRLANT 126 (Göttingen: Vandenhoeck & Ruprecht, 1982), p. 184.
50. In other words, that "Christians [were] liked by the whole (Jewish) people" (Ernst Haenchen, *The Acts of the Apostles* [Philadelphia: Westminster, 1971], p. 193)!
51. Ibid., p. 189. "We misuse Luke's account . . . when we make believe . . . it offers us a documentary film of the beginnings of the Christian mission" (ibid.).
52. By "*under*represented," I have in mind relative rather than absolute numbers; the relative proportion of Jewish Christians would have appeared inordinately low not only compared to Gentile Christians but also compared to what was hoped for vis-à-vis Jews per se.
53. Teeple, "Beginnings," pp. 109, 120. Cf. his argumentation, pp. 108ff.
54. Cf. 2 Cor. 11:24; also especially note 4, above.
55. These reflect early rationales Jews may have brought against Jewish-Christian claims. E.g.: *Issue:* Elijah has not come (cf. Mark 9:11; *attempted solution:* cf. 9:13; Matt. 17:13). *Issue:* Jesus' crucifixion disconfirms his messianic credentials (*apparent responses:* cf. Mark 10:33f. [he *expected* execution]; Matt. 26:53 [he *chose* not to prevent it]; Matt. 26:54 [he had to fulfill Scripture]). *Issue:* the resurrection did not occur (*response:* cf. Mark 16:1-8; *further response:* cf. Matt. 27:62-66; 28:4, 11-15). While the Gospels are late, these issues appear to be early. Cf. notes 56–57 below.
56. I.e., Christians of the apostolic period, urgently in need of guidance as to how they might respond to "Pharisees" of their day.
57. Cf. Martin Albertz, *Die Synoptischen Streitgespräche* (Berlin: Trowitzsch, 1921); Burton Scott Easton, *The Gospel before the Gospels* (New York: Charles Scribner's Sons, 1928), pp. 71ff.; Rudolf Bultmann, *The History of the Synoptic Tradition,* trans. John Marsh (New York: Harper & Row, 1968), p. 321, note 2; Vincent Taylor, *The Formation of the Gospel Tradition,* 2nd ed. (London: Macmillan, 1935), pp. 15-17, 87; Cook, *Mark's Treatment,* chap. 3; Arland J. Hultgren, *Jesus and His Adversaries: The Form and Function of the Conflict Stories in the Synoptic Tradition* (Minneapolis: Augsburg, 1979), chap. 5.
58. Wilson, *Gentile Mission,* agreeing that the numbers are exaggerated (p. 232), feels Luke would not "perpetrate deliberate falsehoods" (p. 261). If, rather than knowingly "recasting," Luke thought his portrait accurate, this would not render his account any the more reliable.
59. Ibid., pp. 232-233: "Most important . . . is not that some accepted [the gospel], but that many rejected it." Thus, to "overemphasise the references to the conversion of the Jews . . . [is to get] hold of the wrong end of the stick!"
60. Luke has Jesus and Jewish followers, including Paul, express continuity with Judaism through abiding by Jewish practice and custom (as illustrated). When Christian ranks later become Gentile, the particulars of Jewish practice and custom cannot, of course, be presented as meaningfully applicable to Gentiles the same way they were to Jesus and Paul (cf. Acts 15).
61. Cf. Acts 10:22 (a "God-fearing man . . . well spoken of *by the . . . Jewish nation*"); 13:16 (Pisidian Antioch's *synagogue:* "Men of Israel, *and* you that fear God"); 13:26 ("brethren . . . of Abraham, *and* those . . . that fear God"); 17:4-5 (Thessalonica's *synagogue:* Jews "were persuaded . . . [*also*] devout Greeks"); 17:12 (Beroea's *synagogue:* Jews "believed, *with* not a few

Greek[s]"); 17:17 ("[Paul] argued in the [Athens] *synagogue* with . . . Jews *and* . . . devout persons"); 18:4 (Corinth's *synagogue:* "persuaded Jews *and* Greeks"). Such Gentiles were "quasi-converts . . . who worshipped the Jewish God, sought to live by the Torah, and attended synagogue . . . but . . . had not submitted to circumcision and thus become full converts . . . [a definition] not without its problems" (Sanders, *Jews,* p. 137).

62. A. Thomas Kraabel, "The Disappearance of the 'God-fearers,' " *Numen* 28 (1981): 113-26. I do not share his skepticism concerning their historical existence.

63. "Christianity is becoming . . . a gentile religion, [its] outreach . . . legitimized by the broad based 'existence' of . . . God-fearers surrounding . . . synagogues of the Diaspora . . . . [God-fearers are] a device to show how Christianity had legitimately become a gentile religion, without losing its roots in . . . Israel" (Robert S. MacLennan and A. Thomas Kraabel, "The God-Fearers—A Literary and Theological Invention," *BARev* 12, no. 5 [1986]: 52).

64. Contra MacLennan and Kraabel; see Robert F. Tannenbaum, "Jews and God-Fearers in the Holy City of Aphrodite," and Louis H. Feldman, "The Omnipresence of the God-Fearers," *BARev* 12, no. 5 (1986): 55-69.

65. The "one, but only one respect," in which Kraabel's argument requires modification (so John G. Gager, "Jews, Gentiles, and Synagogues in the Book of Acts," in *Christians among Jews and Gentiles,* ed. George W. E. Nickelsburg [Philadelphia: Fortress, 1986], p. 98).

66. MacLennan and Kraabel, "God-Fearers," 53. That Godfearers serve a transitional function is evinced by their placement only in the middle chapters of Acts (cf. note 61 above).

67. Jack T. Sanders, "The Salvation of the Jews in Luke-Acts," in *Luke-Acts: New Perspectives from the Society of Biblical Literature Seminar,* ed. Charles H. Talbert (New York: Crossroad, 1984), p. 112 (the emphasis is Sanders').

68. Jervell, *People of God,* p. 46, correctly notes: "When James in 21:20 speaks of tens of thousands of believing Jews . . . he is talking about Jerusalem, as is clear from v. 22"; paradoxically, Jervell also applies 21:20 to a continuing successful post-Judean mission (noted by Sanders, *Jews,* p. 283 and p. 391, note 39).

69. In Matthew, e.g., while the disciples are early instructed to go only to Israel (10:5-6; 15:24), an ultimate intent is to justify Christianity's turn to Gentiles (because the Jews refused the mission's original direction). The Great Commission (28:19ff.), ending Matthew, neutralizes 10:5-6 and 15:24, now defining the Christian mission as being to all nations, not Israel alone (or, if "nations" = "Gentiles," not Israel at all!). See Douglas R. A. Hare, "Make Disciples of All the Gentiles (Mt. 28:19)," *CBQ* 37 (1975):359-369; Kenneth W. Clark, "The Gentile Bias in Matthew," *JBL* 66 (1947):166. While Matthew and Acts are, of course, significantly different works, they both illustrate how early, seemingly pro-Jewish sentiments (in Acts, success with "myriads"), may culminate in negative judgments. Cf. Michael J. Cook, "Interpreting 'Pro-Jewish' Passages in Matthew," *HUCA* 54 (1983):135-147.

70. Luke 4:25ff., referring to 1 Kings 18:1-9 and 2 Kings 5:1-14. The episode is anti-Jewish also because "the people from Nazareth [seeking to throw him over the cliff] . . . become the example of all Jews" (Walter Schmithals, *Das Evangelium nach Lukas,* Zürcher Bibelkommentar [Zurich: Theologischer Verlag, 1980], p. 62).

71. Cf. section II, below.
72. Cf. Wilson, *Gentile Mission*, p. 251: "Whereas Paul clearly hopes for the ultimate salvation of Israel, the impression left by Luke is that the Jews are lost forever."
73. Sanders, "Salvation," p. 116 (emphasis added).
74. Haenchen, *Acts*, p. 102. Conversions of individual Jews reflect other concerns not bearing on the question of a continuing mission to Jews in Luke's day: (1) "the gospel cannot be powerless, and so a few Jews are saved along the way"; (2) "although the *period* of Jewish salvation is over, individual Jews may still be saved . . . if they . . . believe (. . . this will increasingly become an oddity)"; (3) since Luke knows of some Diaspora Jewish Christians, he can hardly "make it appear that the gospel . . . was received only by Gentiles. [Such] Jewish salvation . . . , however, is incidental . . . not the principal motif . . . Jervell, Lohfink and their followers maintain" (Sanders, *Jews*, pp. 250-251, 264). Even Jervell agrees that, at the end of Acts, the mission to Jews is over, and the time of the Gentile mission begins, this being "the time of Luke" (*Luke and the People of God*, p. 68).
75. "The fault lay not with the church but with the Jews . . . [who had] persistently refused the gospel. Paul did not reject the Jews; rather, they rejected him" (Wilson, *Gentile Mission*, p. 247).
76. The parable of the great supper (Luke 14:16ff.), 14:24.
77. G. W. Trompf, "On Why Luke Declined to Recount the Death of Paul: Acts 27-28 and Beyond," in *Luke-Acts: New Perspectives*, pp. 227ff.
78. Ibid., p. 228: "Those who unjustly oppose the new movement . . . [are] rejected by God, whose oracles are quoted against them by Lucan heroes. The ruin of the Jewish nation had already been forecast by Jesus, and the New Testament nowhere more clearly pronounced this awesome fate than in Luke's works." Cf. Beck, *Mature Christianity*, pp. 207, 241: "The anti-Jewish polemic in Acts . . . is the most . . . destructive of Judaism in all of the New Testament documents."
79. Luke 20:17-18. More scathing, in Sanders' view (*Jews*, p. 61), is the parable of the pounds (Luke 19:12-27): "The nobleman is Jesus, his kingdom is the Kingdom of God, those who send an embassy seeking to thwart his accession to dominion over them . . . are the Jews, and the execution of these rebels upon the return of the nobleman now become king . . . is the well-merited destruction of the Jews at the Second Coming."
80. Cf. Wilson, *Gentile Mission*, p. 251.
81. I note my appreciation to Judith Wentling and Waverly Nunnally for their suggestions concerning this essay.

Chapter 8. Joseph B. Tyson, "The Problem of Jewish Rejection in Acts"

1. Acts 28:30-31 does not report an incident but rather functions as a summary of a two-year period of Paul's activities in Rome.
2. Paul's statement in Acts 28:18-19 is not quite consistent with the procedure described earlier in Acts. Paul's appeal to Caesar came during his trial before Festus when he was given the alternative to be tried in Jerusalem (Acts 25:9-12). At a later hearing Festus and Agrippa express the judgment that Paul is innocent (26:31-32).

NOTES

3. Cf. especially Jacob Jervell, "The Divided People of God," in *Luke and the People of God* (Minneapolis: Augsburg, 1972), pp. 41-74. For specific reference to the ending of Acts, cf. pp. 63-69.
4. Cf. Robert C. Tannehill, "Rejection by Jews and Turning to Gentiles: The Pattern of Paul's Mission in Acts," chap. 6 above. Cf. also his "Israel in Luke-Acts: A Tragic Story," *JBL* 104 (1985): 69-85.
5. Cf. Ernst Haenchen, "Judentum und Christentum in der Apostelgeschichte," *ZNW* 54 (1963): 155-187; cf. also his commentary, *The Acts of the Apostles*, trans. Bernard Noble and Gerald Shinn (Oxford: Basil Blackwell, 1971), pp. 721-732. A similar position has been maintained by Stephen G. Wilson, *The Gentiles and the Gentile Mission in Luke-Acts*, SNTSMS 23 (Cambridge: At the University Press, 1973), pp. 219-238; and "The Jews and the Death of Jesus in Acts," in *Anti-Judaism in Early Christianity*, ed. Peter Richardson (Waterloo: Wilfrid Laurier University Press, 1986), 1:155-164. Cf. also the careful work of Lloyd Gaston, "Anti-Judaism and the Passion Narrative in Luke and Acts," in ibid., 1:127-153. Cf. also Jack T. Sanders, "The Salvation of the Jews in Luke-Acts," in *Luke-Acts: New Perspectives from the Society of Biblical Literature Seminar*, ed. Charles H. Talbert (New York: Crossroad, 1984), pp. 104-128; Jack T. Sanders, "The Jewish People in Luke-Acts," chap. 4 above; Robert L. Maddox, *The Purpose of Luke-Acts* (Edinburgh: T. & T. Clark, 1982), especially pp. 31-65. Robert L. Brawley takes a mediating position in "Paul in Acts: Lucan Apology and Conciliation," in *Luke-Acts: New Perspectives*, pp. 129-147.
6. Cf. Haenchen, *Acts of the Apostles*, pp. 721-732, for an analysis of other exegetical problems.
7. Nils Dahl, "A People for His Name," *NTS* 4 (1958):319-327. Dahl lists only two exceptions: Acts 15:14; 18:10.
8. The ambivalence of Luke's treatment of the Jews is recognized by Wilson, "The Jews and the Death of Jesus," and *The Gentiles*, pp. 219-38, as well as by Gaston, "Anti-Judaism and the Passion," and Maddox, *Purpose of Luke-Acts*. Gaston writes: "In any case the paradox remains that Luke-Acts is one of the most pro-Jewish and one of the most anti-Jewish writings in the New Testament" (p. 153).
9. Cf. especially Acts 9:15, where Paul is designated as missionary both to Gentiles and Israel; 11:18, the recognition that God has granted repentance to Gentiles; and the three Pauline announcements, 13:46; 18:6; 28:28.
10. On Passover, cf. Luke 2:41; 22:1,8,11,13,15; Acts 12:4. Luke uses the term "unleavened bread" interchangably with "Passover" in Luke 22:1,7; Acts 12:3; 20:6. On Pentecost, cf. Acts 2:1; 20:16.
11. On the differences between Pharisees and Sadducees, cf. especially Acts 23:6-10. Chief priests, priests, scribes, and elders are referred to frequently in Luke 22:66—23:25 and elsewhere.
12. Cf., e.g., Acts 2:16,29-31; 4:25-28; 8:32-35; 13:33-41.
13. This continuity is stressed by Jervell, "The Divided People of God."
14. It may be correct to understand the identification of Alexander as Jewish in 19:34 as pejorative, but on the part of the Ephesians, not Luke. In the narrative, it is stated that when the crowd recognized that Alexander was a Jew, he was prevented from speaking.
15. Cf. Joseph B. Tyson, *The Death of Jesus in Luke-Acts* (Columbia: University of South Carolina Press, 1986), pp. 48-83. Cf. also Gaston, "Anti-Judaism and the Passion."

16. To speak of characteristic use does not mean that Luke's use of the plural is without variation. A major exception to the general rule is found in Acts 16:20, where Paul and Silas are designated as Jews. Moreover, a reference such as the address to Jews in 2:14 has no suggestion of enmity.
17. Stephen's words reflect Isa. 63:10 and perhaps also Isa. 6:9-10, the verses quoted in Acts 28:26-27.
18. The community starts with a handful in Acts 1:13-14, adds 120 in 1:15, 3000 in 2:41, and totals around 5000 in 4:4.
19. Cf. Acts 1:14; 2:43-47; 4:32-37; 5:12-16.
20. Cf. Haenchen, *Acts of the Apostles,* pp. 343-363.
21. Cf. Joseph B. Tyson, "The Gentile Mission and the Authority of Scripture in Acts," *NTS* 33 (1987): 619-631.
22. Cf. the description in Acts 10:12 of the foods that Peter is commanded to eat: "all kinds of animals and reptiles and birds of the air."
23. Jervell maintains that the power of this conservative minority in the church lies behind the composition of Acts and requires the author to present Paul as a loyal Jew. Cf. Jacob Jervell, "The Mighty Minority," in *The Unknown Paul* (Minneapolis: Augsburg, 1984), pp. 26-51. Cf. also his "The History of Early Christianity and the Acts of the Apostles," in ibid., pp. 13-25.